White Peak Aircraft Wreck Walks

by John N. Merrill

Maps, sketches and photographs by John N. Merrill

"I hike the paths and trails of the world for others to enjoy."

© *John N. Merrill 2004*

Walk & Write Ltd.

The Aircraft Wreck Walks Series.

2004

Walk & Write Ltd.,
Marathon House,
Longcliffe, Nr. Matlock,
Derbyshire, England. DE4 4HN

Tel/Fax 01629 - 540991
email - marathonhiker@aol.com

Typeset and designed by John N. Merrill & Walk & Write Ltd.
Printed and handmade by John N. Merrill.

©Text - - John N. Merrill, HonMUniv. 2004.
© Photographs, Maps & sketches - John N. Merrill, HonMUniv, 2004.
ISBN 1-903627-49-4
First published - February 2004.

British Library Cataloguing-in-Publication Data. A catalogue record of this book is available from the British Library.

Typeset in Arial, italic, and plain 11pt, 14pt and 18pt by J. Merrill

Please note - The maps in this guide are purely illustrative. You are encouraged to use the appropriate 1:25,000 O.S. map.

John N. Merrill has walked all the routes in this book. Meticulous research has been undertaken to ensure that this publication is highly accurate at the time of going to press. The publishers, however, cannot be held responsible for alterations, errors, omissions, or for changes in details given. They would welcome information to help keep the book up to date.

Cover design and photographs - by John N. Merrill
- Walk & Write Ltd 2004

A little about John N. Merrill

Few people have walked the earth's crust more than John Merrill with more than 180,000 miles in the last 32 years - the average person walks 75,000 miles in a lifetime. Apart from walking too much causing bones in his feet to snap, like metal fatigue, he has never suffered from any back, hip or knee problems. Like other walkers he has suffered from many blisters, his record is 23 on both feet! He wears out at least three pairs of boots a year and his major walking has cost over £125,000. This includes 100 pairs of boots costing more than £11,800 and over £1,900 on socks - a pair of socks last three weeks and are not washed!

His marathon walks in Britain include - -

Hebridean Journey....... 1,003 miles. Northern Isles Journey......913 miles.
Irish Island Journey ....1,578 miles.   Parkland Journey.......2,043 miles.
Land's End to John o' Groats.....1,608 miles.
The East of England Heritage Route - 450miles.

and in 1978 he became the first person to walk the entire coastline of Britain - 6,824 miles in ten months.

In Europe he has walked across Austria - 712 miles - hiked the Tour of Mont Blanc, the Normandy coast, the Loire Valley (450 miles), a high level route across the Augverne(230 miles) and the River Seine (200 miles) in France, completed High Level Routes in the Dolomites and Italian Alps, and the GR20 route across Corsica in training! Climbed the Tatra Mountains ,the Transylvanian Alps in Romania, and in Germany walked in the Taunus, Rhine, the Black Forest (Clock Carriers Way) and King Ludwig Way (Bavaria). He has walked across Europe - 2,806 miles in 107 days - crossing seven countries, the Swiss and French Alps and the complete Pyrennean chain - the hardest and longest mountain walk in Europe, with more than 600,000 feet of ascent! In 1998 he walked 1,100 miles along the pilgrimage route from Le Puy (France) to Santiago (Spain) and onto Cape Finisterre; in 2002 walked 700 miles from Seville to Santiago de Compostela. In 2003 he walked 650 miles through the length of Portual via Fatima to Santiago de Compostela (Spian); 400 miles from Oslo to Trondheim, following St. Olav's Way, and all the trails on the Hong Kong Islands.

In America he used The Appalachian Trail - 2,200 miles - as a training walk, before walking from Mexico to Canada via the Pacific Crest Trail in record time - 118 days for 2,700 miles. Recently he walked most of the Continental Divide Trail and much of New Mexico; his second home. In 1999 he walked the Chesopeake & Ohio Canal National Historical Trail. In 2,000 he became the first thru hiker to walk 1,340 miles around Ohio, following the Buckeye Trail. In Canada he has walked the Rideau Trail - Kingston to Ottowa - 220 miles and The Bruce Trail - Tobermory to Niagara Falls - 460 miles.

In 1984 John set off from Virginia Beach on the Atlantic coast, and walked 4,226 miles without a rest day, across the width of America to Santa Cruz and San Francisco on the Pacific coast. This is one of the finest and most memorable walks, being in modern history, the longest, hardest crossing of the U.S.A. in the shortest time - under six months (178 days). The direct distance is 2,800 miles.

Between major walks John is out training in his own area - The Peak District National Park. He has walked all of our National Trails many times - The Cleveland Way thirteen times and The Pennine Way four times in a year! He has been trekking in the Himalayas five times. He created more than thirty-five challenge walks which have been used to raise more than £600,000 for charity. From his own walks he has raised over £100,000. He is author of more than 225 walking guides which he prints and publishes himself, His book sales are in excess of 3 million, He has created many long distance walks including The Limey Way, The Peakland Way, Dark Peak Challenge walk, Rivers' Way, The Belvoir Witches Challenge Walk, The Forest of Bowland Challenge. the Dore to New Mills Challenge Walk , the Lincolnshire Wolds "Black Death" Challenge Walk and the Happy Hiker (White Peak) Challenge Walk. His new Pilgrim Walk Series includes the 72 mile, "Walsingham Way" - Ely to Walsingham. His monthly walks appear in Derbyshire's "Reflections" magazine. In January 2003, he was honoured for his walking and writing, recieving a Honorary degree, Master of the University, from Derby University.

CONTENTS

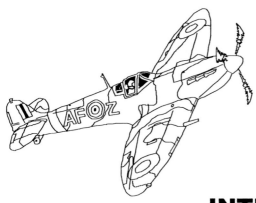

INTRODUCTION

This whole book started by accident. A few months ago I was walking through Middleton by Youlgreave and noticed a plaque to a bomber that came down at Smerrill. I was familiar to the Dark Peak wrecks but had been oblivious to any in the lower peak. So my research began and as they say ......the result has been this book! It is strange how life twists and turns. I was adopted and lived in Sheffield and all I knew was that my natural father had been killed over Germany in the last war - I always fantasised it was the Dam Busters raid. It was only recently I learnt that my natural father had been in the RAF but died, many years later, from natural causes.

My adopted father was a brilliant chemical engineer and in later life was a close friend of Arthur Rubbra, the man behind the Merlin engine in the Spitfire. How strange that I found in my fathers papers photos and research on Mr. Rubbra, who I had often met! Yet a further twist the overall story was this Middleton bomber was well known to a friend, now dead, who had been a friend for years camping at his farm. He had been in the Home Guard and actually helped at the rescue. Whilst I never recall him mentioning it, his wife has informed me it was his favourite story, which he loved to recall! One final twist was for a while I lived in Ripley, doors away from where Sir Barnes Wallis was born, the creator of the famous "bouncing bomb". I often walked through the park there which bears his name, just off Moseley Street.

The exploration of the walks and the research has been fascinating. It is not from a morbid sense of view but a historical one, for here is recent history. I have found most of the sites, seen the craters or found pieces of metal still on the site. Many have nothing to be seen, others are on Private land. Any remains are Crown property and should not be removed. Furthermore it is exciting to find a part of the scene and leave it for others to discover. Remember also the sites are the "resting places" to some brave air crews.

The research has been scanty for during World War 11, the newspapers did not carry any stories of these crashes, fearing it would jeopardise our war effort. Some of the leads have been word of mouth and whilst this is the book at this stage, I believe it is an on going story as more leads are offered to me. So with each new edition it will grow! I would welcome any information for further editions.

The walks take you on the nearest right of way to the site but as many are on Private Land, the exact location is not given. Details of the plane are given to get a more complete picture. To complete the military aircraft content of the book I have included a Dam Busters walk around Derwent and Howden Reservoirs. The title of the book is a slight misnomer but I wanted to cover sites away from the moorland masses of Kinder and Bleaklow. As a result I have wandered into gritstone country and ended up further south than I expected.

Happy walking

Alan W Mewull

Acknowlegment

Such a book as this relies on help from many people - the walking is the easy bit! I am particularly grateful to the Ministry of Defence (AHB3 (RAF) - Room 308, who have provided me with names of the various air crews and some details of the accident. To the Leek and District Historical Society who provided me with information on the crashes in their area. My thanks to the Derby, Chesterfield, Matlock, Leek and Sheffield Libraries (Local History Departments) who have found answers to my questions. Finally to many people I have met in the field who pointed me in the right direction or recalled seeing the plane. Combined they have helped to make this project not just a walking experience but a very rewarding experience.

ABOUT THE WALKS

Whilst every care is taken detailing and describing the walk in this book, it should be borne in mind that the countryside changes by the seasons and the work of man. I have described the walk to the best of my ability, detailing what I have found on the walk in the way of stiles and signs. Obviously with the passage of time stiles become broken or replaced by a ladder stile or even a small gate. Signs too have a habit of being broken or pushed over. All the route follow rights of way and only on rare occasions will you have to overcome obstacles in its path, such as a barbed wire fence or electric fence. On rare occasions rights of way are rerouted and these ammendments are included in the next edition.

The seasons bring occasional problems whilst out walking which should also be borne in mind. In the height of summer paths become overgrown and you will have to fight your way through in a few places. In low lying areas the fields are often full of crops, and although the pathline goes straight across it may be more practical to walk round the field edge to get to the next stile or gate. In summer the ground is generally dry but in autumn and winter, especially because of our climate, the surface can be decidedly wet and slippery; sometimes even gluttonous mud!

These comments are part of countryside walking which help to make your walk more interesting or briefly frustrating. Standing in a farmyard up to your ankles in mud might not be funny at the time but upon reflection was one of the highlights of the walk!

The mileage for each section is based on three calculations -

1. pedometer reading.
2. the route map measured on the map.
3. the time I took for the walk.

I believe the figure stated for each section to be very accurate but we all walk differently and not always in a straight line! The time allowed for each section is on the generous side and does not include pub stops etc. The figure is based on the fact that on average a person walks 2 1/2 miles an hours but less in hilly terrain.

ROD MOOR - 5 MILES

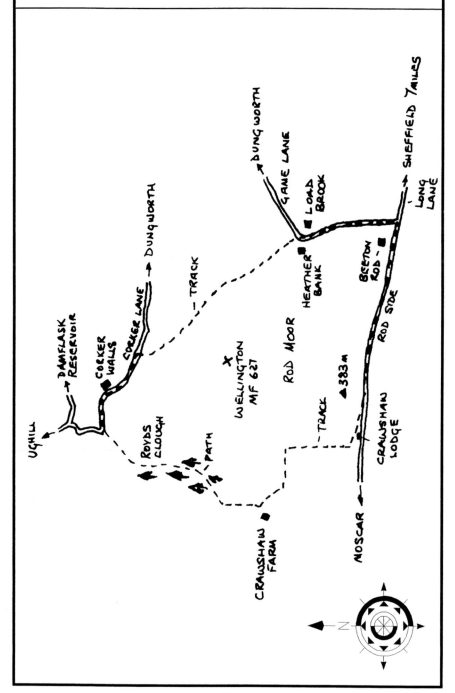

ROD MOOR
- 5 MILES
- allow 2 hours.

Route - Long Lane - Rod Side - Crawshaw Lodge - Crawshaw Farm - Royds Clough - Corker Walls - Corker Lane - Hall Broom - Load Brook - Beeton Green - Long Lane.

  - 1:25,000 Outdoor Leisure map - The Dark Peak.

VISITOR PARKING *- None. Roadside only. Junction of Beeton Green and Long Lane - 7 miles from Sheffield. Grid Ref. 273881.*

 - None!

ABOUT THE WALK - On Rod Moor a Vickers Wellington No. MF627 crashed on 22nd October 1942. The walk takes you along the nearest right of way to the site, which is on private land. The actual walk is a delight and quite a superb short walk on the edge of the Peak District National Park, with views over South Yorkshire to Sheffield, Bradfield and Damflask Reservoir.

WALKING INSTRUCTIONS - From the road junction head westwards along the lane past Rod Side, with Rod Moor to your right. In little over 1/2 mile reach the drive to Crawshaw Lodge and path sign. Walk along the drive to the right of the lodge to a gate. Continue ahead on a track which soon turns right over Rod Moor. In less than 1/4 mile, as signed, turn left along the track descending towards Crawshaw Farm. Approaching the gate turn right, at a stile and path sign, and descend the field to the right of the farm to a path sign and a stile. Turn right along a track to the pine trees of Royds Clough. Follow the track round to your right and in a few yards turn right onto a path. This leads through the trees above the clough at first then descends close to the stream, before bearing slightly left keeping a wall on your right to gain at ladder stile on the edge of the woodland. Over this cross the field to the far righthand corner where there is a kissing gate. Continue along the field edge to a stile and path sign before Corker Lane.

Turn right along the lane passing Corker Walls farm on your left. Keep on the lane for 1/4 mile with views to your left to Damflask Reservoir. Reach a track on your right. Turn right to a gate and Bradfield Parish path sign - a feature of this walk. Follow the track which ascends at first but soon levels off. Here to your right can be seen a wall on the moor above - Rod Moor - and it is in that area the plane came down. Continue on the track with the wall on your left to a stile. Continue ahead to another and here gain a tarmaced track. Follow this to the lane above the hamlet of Load Brook. Turn right and descend through the hamlet, along Beeton Green, and ascend gently back to the road junction, where you began.

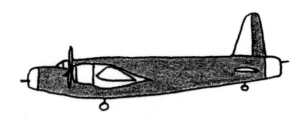

THE VICKERS WELLINGTON BOMBER -
BRITISH MADE AND DATES FROM 1940 AND USED AS A LONG RANGE BOMBER, PRIMARILY ON NIGHT RAIDS.
POWERED BY TWO 1,000 HP BRITISH PEGASUS XVIII ENGINES.
MAX SPEED - 235M.P.H. (378KM). AT 15,500 FT.
RATE OF CLIMB - 1,120 FEET PER MINUTE.
CEILING HEIGHT - 18,000 FEET.
RANGE - 1,200 MILES.
WINGSPAN - 86' 2" (26.3M.)
LENGTH - 64' 7" (19.7M.)
ARMAMENTS -
NOSE TURRET - 2 .303 MACHINE GUNS
TAIL TURRET - 2 .303 MACHINE GUNS.

Rod Moor and view to Damflask Reservoir.

Vickers Wellington MF627 - 6ANS
Crashed 22nd October 1942
Crew -
Sgt R.A. Keith 1606011 (uninjured)
Plt Off D.E. Ward 2527615 (injured).
Plt Off Thirkell (No initial or number available) (Uninjured).

Whilst carrying out "GEE" letdown, the aircraft struck high ground. Only one of the crew was injured.

A brief report with wreckage photographs is detailed in the Sheffield Telegraph, dated 23rd October 1952. The RAF Wellington bomber crashed in heavy mist on Hall Broom Pasture (north of Rod Moor.). The crew of three suffered minor injuries. The plane was completely wrecked and tore down a 70 yards section of wall near the summit of the hill. The nose of the aircraft was flung over 50 yards. The crew crawled out, Pilot Officer David Edward Ward (19) had a suspected broken jaw. Pilot, Sgt. Reginald A. Keith, walked down to Corkerwalls Farm, to get help. Both he and Pilot Officer Brian Thinkwell (19) had a broken finger. The plane was on a cross country training flight from RAF Lichfield, Staffordshire.

CROW CHIN - 4 MILES

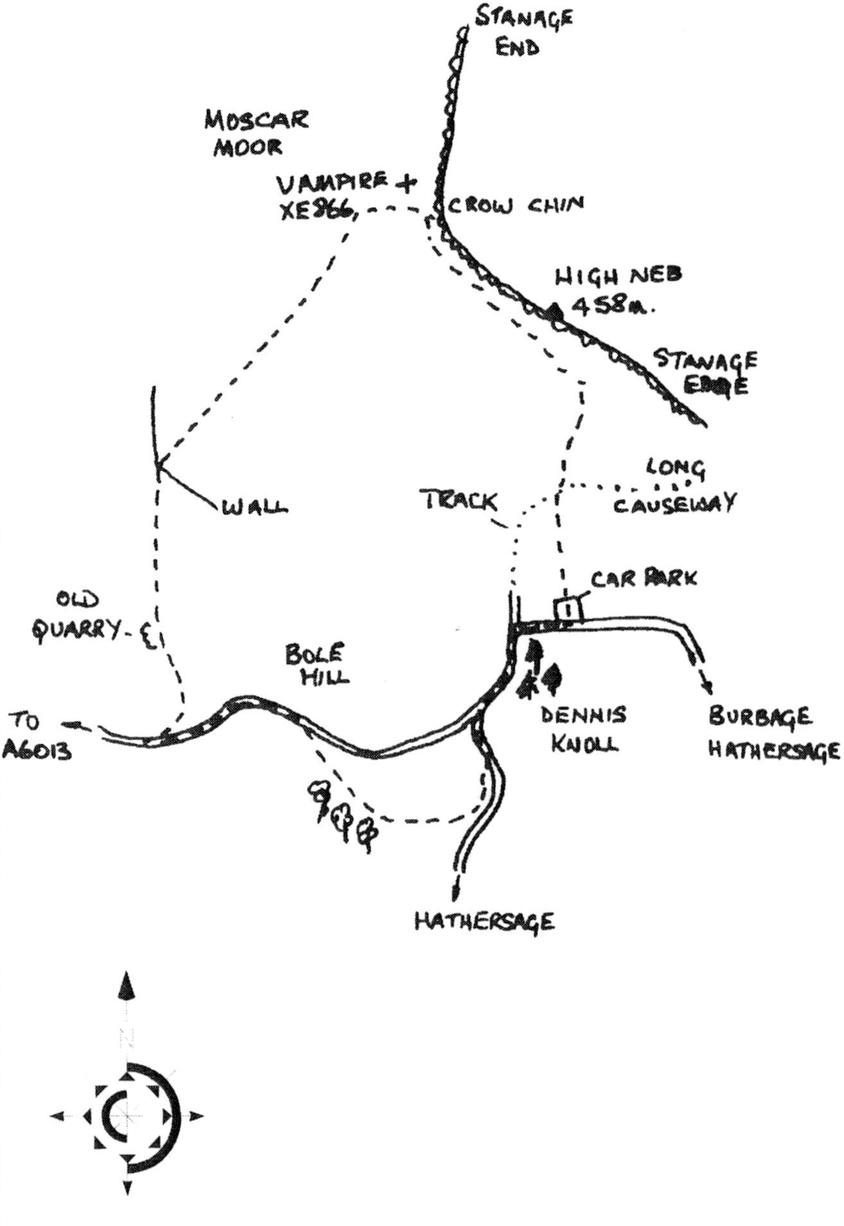

STANAGE
END

MOSCAR
MOOR

VAMPIRE +
XE866,

CROW CHIN

HIGH NEB
458m.

STANAGE
EDGE

LONG
CAUSEWAY

WALL

TRACK

CAR PARK

OLD
QUARRY-

BOLE
HILL

DENNIS
KNOLL

BURBAGE
HATHERSAGE

TO
A6013

HATHERSAGE

N

CROW CHIN
- 4 MILES
- allow 2 hours.

Route - Dennis Knoll - Bolehill Wood - Disused Quarry - Bamford Moor - Moscar Moor - Crow Chin - Stanage Edge - Dennis Knoll.

 – 1:25,000 Outdoor Leisure Map - The Dark Peak - East Sheet.

VISITOR PARKING *- Small parking area opposite Dennis Knoll wood at the junction of the track - Long Causeway - to Stanage Pole. Grid Ref. 227844.*

 - None. Nearest in Hathersage or Bamford.

ABOUT THE WALK -A delightful walk across the moorland to Crow Chin area of Stanage Edge. The path is little used and in clear weather the routes destination is obvious, but it is prudent to go by compass across here. Below Crow Chin on Moscar Moor a De Havilland Vampire No. XE866, crashed on August 8th 1957. Near Strines inn another Vampire No.WA400 made a forced landing on 25th July 1951. The site is on private land - part of the Fitzwilliam Wentworth Estates. However, the Strines Inn is an impressive refreshment point after the walk and to get there by road you pass the Ladybower Inn, which has as its sign the Dam Busters practising on the Derwent Dams, and is in memory of the famous 617 squadron.

The walk is full of interest and as you walk beneath Stanage Edge you will see some of the hundreds of millstones lying around. A local industry that ceased last century.

WALKING INSTRUCTIONS - From the car park head southwards along the road towards Bamford/Ladybower. Cross a cattle grid and keep Dennis Knoll wood on your left. In 200 yards turn left along the road - the road right goes over Bole Hill which you will join soon, on the other side of the hill. A short distance down the road turn right at the first stile and path sign on your right. The path parallels the road at first before swinging right and keeping you to the righthand side of trees. In less than 1/2 mile gain the road from Bole Hill, via a stile beside a pathsign. Turn left and follow the lane around to your left to summit of the road. Here you have splendid views of the Hope Valley. In a few yards later turn right at the stile and path sign. At first the path is well defined as you ascend to your right, at first, before swinging left to the righthand side of a small quarry. Here bear slightly right and follow a compass bearing, basically due north. In 1/4 mile reach the corner of a partially broken wall. Here bearing slightly right again and now with Crow Chin area of Stanage Edge clearly in view, follow a compass bearing - 48 degrees - towards the rocks. In 1/2 mile cross the top of Jarvis Clough area of Moscar Moor. Here on your left is where the Vampire crashed.

Ascend towards the rocks where you pick up the main path beneath Stanage Edge. Turn right along this passing many millstone and in 1/2 mile, just past the High Neb area of Stanage Edge, turn right and descend the path to a stile and track - Long Causeway. Turn right and follow the track down to the car park.

DEHAVILLAND VAMPIRE -
POWERED BY ONE 3,000LB D.H.GOBLIN ENGINE.
WING SPAN - 40'
LENGTH - 30' 9"
MAX SPEED - 540 MPH AT 20,000 FEET.
RATE OF CLIMB - 4,200 FEET ME MINUTE.
RANGE - 730 MILES
ARMAMENTS - 4 X 30MM FUSELAGE NOSE.

DeHavilland Vampire XE866 - 4FTS
Crashed - Moscar Moor - August 8th 1957.
Crew -
Fg Off P.R.Green 4091376
Fg Off D.J.Brett 4039420

The cause of the crash is uncertain and both of the crew were killed.

CROW CHIN (Stanage). Re DeHavilland Vampire XE866-4FTS.
Photos of the crash and search are detailed in the Sheffield Telegraph 9th August 1957. The plane took off from Worksop at 8.35am on its return, 12 miles from Worksop the Pilot radioed he was short of fuel and losing height. Was told to descend to 6,000 ft. and fly a certain bearing but as a Derbyshire Police Officer reported, "It would appear that the Pilot got away from the built up area of Sheffield before crashing". An all day search was organised by the RAF rescue team from Harpur Hill, Buxton. The Strines Inn was set up as a rescue headquarters. In late evening the wreckage was found and two bodies. The plane had crashed into a rock face at 1,400 ft. with the wreckage spread over the Derbyshire and Yorkshire boundary. The force of the impact cut the bodies in half.

DeHavilland Vampire WA400 - 102FRS
Crashed - nr Strines - July 25th 1951
Crew -
Fg Off L.L.Beckford 205417.

The pilot was on a training flight and became lost. Being low on fuel he made a forced landing on the moorland and was uninjured.

Crow Chin and the crash site on Moscar Moor.

OVER HADDON - 4 MILES

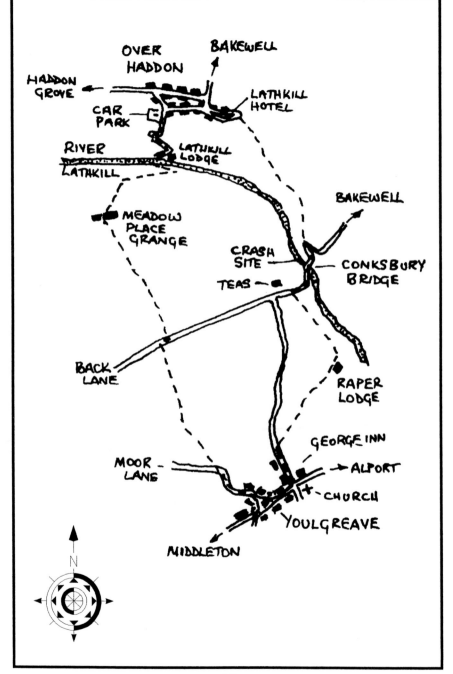

OVER HADDON & YOULGREAVE
- 4 miles
- allow 2 hours.

Route - Over Haddon - Conksbury Bridge - Lathkill Dale - Raper Lodge - Youlgreave - Meadow Place Grange - Lathkill Dale - Over Haddon.

 - 1:25,000 Outdoor Leisure Map - The White Peak - East Sheet.

 - Over Haddon.

 - Lathkill Hotel, Over Haddon. Several in Youlgreave.

 - Geoffs Diner, Over Haddon. Outside tearoom near Conksbury Bridge.

ABOUT THE WALK - My information on this crash site is scanty. I am informed by a very reliable source, that a fighter plane crashed into the River Lathkill just before Conksbury Bridge. Remarkably the plane landed on the fishermans bank in the middle of the river. On standing on the bridge looking towards Over Haddon the bank is clearly seen, where the plane came to rest.

The views early on on this walk down onto Lathkill Dale are simply beautiful. You walk a short section of the dale before ascending to Youlgreave with its remarkable church - well worth a visit. You return over the fields to Meadow Place Grange where you descend to the dale before ascending back into Over Haddon. A delightful hilly walk!

WALKING INSTRUCTIONS - From the car park cross the road - which you ascend at the end - and walk through Over Haddon. Where it turns left keep ahead on the small road to the Lathkill Lodge Hotel with footpath stile and sigh beyond. Over this keep right and follow the defined path across the field to a

17

stile and vantage point above Lathkill Dale. Keep above the dale and reaching another stile keep right to gain another close to the road at Conksbury. Descend the road and cross Conksbury Bridge and its fine view up to Over Haddon; the plane landed almost infront of you! Follow the road round to your right and turn left along the footpath down Lathkill Dale. Follow it for just over 1/4 mile to a track with Raper House ahead. Turn right and ascend the track to the road in Youlgreave. Turn left to the inn and church. Turn right along the main street in Youlgreave and opposite the former Co-Op store - now the YHA - turn right past Thimble Hall and follow the road. Keep right shortly afterwards and ascend the road for 1/4 mile to a path sign and track on your right. Turn along this and follow it past a small plantation and stile. Descend the field beyond and ascend the other side to a stile and keep a wall on your right to meet the road from Conksbury.

Turn right for a few yards to a stile and path sign on your left. Turn left and keep the wall on your right to another stile and descend to Meadow Place Grange. Go straight across the farmyard and though the gates to a field beyond. Cross the field keeping slightly right to a gate and track. Here descend the track as it zig-zags down to the stone flagged footbridge in Lathkill Dale. Cross to the other side to Lathkill Lodge and ascend the road back into Over Haddon.

The view from Conksbury Bridge to Over Haddon. In the foreground is the fisherman's bank, in the middle of the river, where the plane came to rest.

18

Remember and observe the Country Code

Enjoy the countryside and respect its life and work.

Guard against all risk of fire.

Fasten all gates.

Keep your dogs under close control.

Keep to public paths across farmland.

Use gates and stiles to cross fences, hedges and walls.

Leave livestock, crops and machinery alone.

Take your litter home - pack it in; pack it out.

Help to keep all water clean.

Protect wildlife, plants and trees.

Take special care on country roads

Make no unnecessary noise.

MIDDLETON & SMERRILL
- 6 MILES

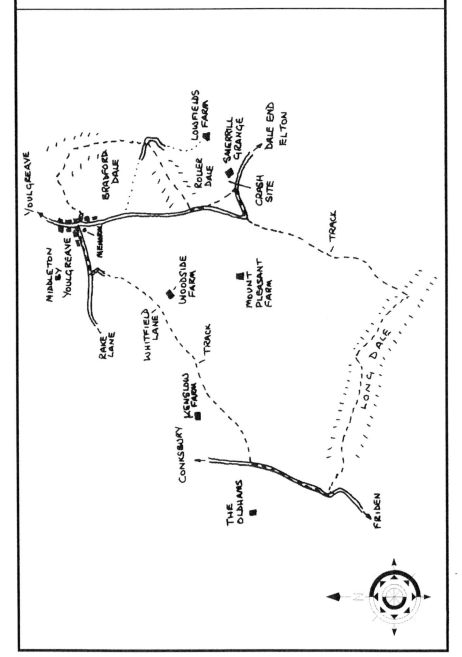

MIDDLETON AND SMERRILL - 6 MILES - allow 2 to 3 hours.

Route - Middleton by Youlgreave - Woodside Farm - Little Rookery Plantation - Long Dale - Smerrill Grange - Roller Dale - Bradford Dale - Middleton by Youlgreave.

 - 1:25,000 Outdoor Leisure Series - The White Peak - East Sheet.

 - None. Roadside parking only.

 - None! Nearest in Youlgreave.

ABOUT THE WALK - In the centre of Middleton are the War Memorial Gardens and on one side of it is a monument to the crew of a Vickers Wellington Mk111 Bomber - RAF No. BJ652 - which crashed at Smerrill Grange on January 21st. 1944. This walk, apart from being a delightful limestone walk, takes you around the Middleton and Smerrill area, where the plane came down. There are no remains to be seen, unlike the sixty or so crashes on the moorlands of the Dark Peak.

WALKING INSTRUCTIONS - From the centre of Middleton, with the entrance to the War Memorial Gardens on your left, walk westwards up the road out of the village. Pass Middleton Hall and Rock Farm on your left. Shortly afterwards walk beside a wood - Rake Wood - on your left and in a few yards turn left on a tarmaced lane. Follow it round to your right and in more than 1/4 mile it turns right to Woodside Farm. Keep straight ahead on a walled track and descend slightly to a gate. Go through and bear right along the track. In 200 yards reach another gate, with the track continuing to Kenslow Farm. Bear left and cross the field to a gap and continue across the next field to a stile. Cross the next field to a more defined stile and onto another. Cross a track to another and cross the centre of the field to a stile and footpath sign beside the road opposite the farm - The Oldhams. Turn left along the road passing the drive to The Oldhams on your right. Gently descend the road to the bend with

Long Dale on your left. Approaching the bend on your left is an old milepost. Walk around the bend before leaving the road on your left to double back on yourself following the walled path in Long Dale.

Follow the walled path for nearly 1/4 mile to its end before continuing straight ahead along the dale floor to a stile by a gate. Continue ahead with the wood on your left to its end by gate. Turn left and ascend above the dale to a small gate on your right. Turn right and walk close to a limestone wall on your left, at first. To your right is Smerrill Moor and below you in Long Dale. The wall turns left but keep straight ahead on the path and in a short distance the wall returns and walk beside it to a gate on your left. Here turn left and keep the wall on your right to a stile and a short section of walled track to another gate. Here on the defined track keep the wall on your left to another gate, here descend to your left to a gate and follow the defined walled path - brideleway - to a road. Turn left and ascend slightly towards Smerrill Grange. It is worth walking a few yards to see it. Little over 1/4 mile further along the road on your left is the site of a Mediaeval village.

Just before the Grange , where the plane came down, at the right-hand bend in the road on your left is a stile on the right-hand side of the gate. Go through here and keep the wall on right as you descend to a stile on your right. Through this walk diagonally right and soon descend steeply to a stile and road. Turn right and in a few yards, as footpath signed and stiled, turn right and walk down Roller Dale. The path is defined and well stiled. Emerging from the dale bear left slightly to reach a stile and road to Lowfield Farm. Cross the road to a stile and continue straight ahead, on the defined stiled path to a stone slab footbridge over the infant River Bradford. Bear left above the river to steps and descend these into Bradford Dale. On your right is the rock where Sir Christopher Fulwood - a royalist - hid in the 17th century before being shot. Remains of his castle can be seen as you enter Middleton, just beyond Castle Farm. Walk through the dale for 200 yards crossing a footbridge, a spring and at the junction of tracks by the ruined mill, turn left and ascend the track back into Middleton, reaching the centre of the village opposite the Wellington Bomber Memorial - Erected by Parish in August 1995, the 50th anniversary of the end of the war. Additonal imformation has been added by me.

In the middle of the year 2,000, fragments of the crashed plane were uncoverd at Smerrill Grange. An eye witness to the crash said the plane exploded on impact throwing the six Royal Australian Air Force crew into the paddock. They were taken to an outbuilding, used as a mortuary. The plane flew low over Youlgreave, heading south up the valley; where the valley turned east, the plane didn't.

MEMORIAL -

In memory of the crew
of Vickers Wellington Mk111Bomber
RAF No. BJ652
which crashed at Smerrill
on January 21st. 1944 at 22.01 hours.

Flt Sgt Lloyd George Edmonds, AUS416941, RAAF, aged 25 - Pilot. - (from Unley, South Australia.)

Flt Sgt Frederick Popsham Deshon, AUS426555, RAAF, aged 27 - Wireless Op. - (from Brisbane, Queensland.)

Sgt Thomas Dudley Murton, AUS426555,RAAF, aged 19 - Air Gunner. - (from Tatura, Victoria.)

Flt Sgt James Kydd, AUS426621, RAAF, aged 26 - Air Bomber. - (from Wynnum, Queensland.)

Flt Sgt William Thomas Barnes, AUS30581, RAAF, aged 27 - Wireless Op.- (from Queensland.)

Flg Offr Keith Jobson Perrett, AUS343608, RAAF, aged 27 - Air Gunner - (from Brisbane, Queensland.)

The surviving records state, "The crew were on a night cross country training flight, when the aircraft struck high ground. The cause of the crash was thought to have been poor interpretation of instruments."

I have subsequently discovered that where I often camped at Dudwood House, near Winster, the occupier, Mr. Jesse Bailey, was in the Home Guard and one of the people who attended the crash scene. His surviving wife informed me that the plane crash was his favourite story.

THE VICKERS WELLINGTON BOMBER -
BRITISH MADE AND DATES FROM 1940 AND USED AS A LONG RANGE BOMBER, PRIMARILY ON NIGHT RAIDS.
POWERED BY TWO 1,000 HP BRITISH PEGASUS XVIII ENGINES.
MAX SPEED - 235M.P.H. (378KM). AT 15,500 FT.
RATE OF CLIMB - 1,120 FEET PER MINUTE.
CEILING HEIGHT - 18,000 FEET.
RANGE - 1,200 MILES.
WINGSPAN - 86' 2" (26.3M.)
LENGTH - 64' 7" (19.7M.)
ARMAMENTS -
NOSE TURRET - 2 .303 MACHINE GUNS.
TAIL TURRET - 2 .303 MACHINE GUNS.

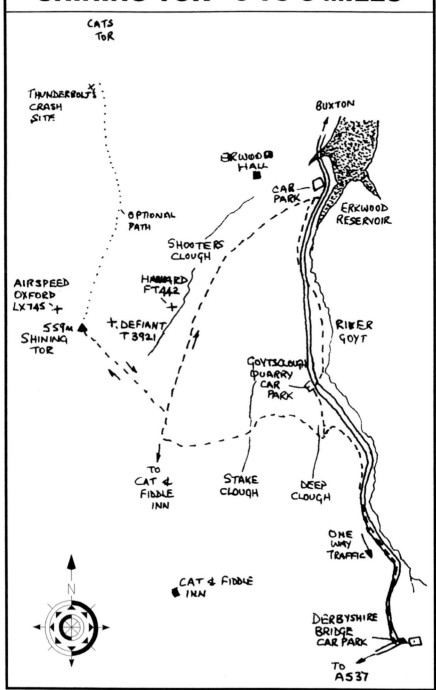

SHINING TOR
- 6 to 8 miles.
- allow 2 to 3 hours.

Route - Derbyshire Bridge - Goyt's Clough - Deep Clough - Stake Clough - Shining Tor - Shooter's Clough - Errwood - Goytsclough Quarry - Goyt's Clough - Derbyshire Bridge.

- 1:25,000 Outdoor Leisure Series - The White Peak - West Sheet.

VISITOR PARKING

- Derbyshire Bridge - reached from A537 (Macclesfield) road. Errwood and Goyts Clough Quarry Car Parks reached via A5004 (Whaley Bridge) road. A one way road system operates in the Goyt Valley.

- None on the route. Nearest is the Cat & fiddle Inn on the A537 (Macclesfield) road.

ABOUT THE WALK - Around the summit of Shining Tor three planes have crashed, and two near Cat's Tor,
1. North American Harvard No. FT442, crashed November 30th 1944.
2. Airspeed Oxford No. LX745, crashed March 12th 1944.
3. Boulton Paul Defiant No. T3921, crashed October 16th 1941.
4. Near the path from Shining Tor towards Cat Tor are two holes on the west side of the slope at GR SK 995754, where two Thunderbolts came down on 18th. October, 1944 (?).

The Goyt Valley is one of the most attractive areas of the National Park, with its mixture of woodland, moorland, lofty vantage points and streams and reservoirs. Whilst I started the walk from the Derbyshire Bridge side - 8 miles, you can start this walk from either Errwood or Goyts Clough Quarry car parks, making it about a six mile walk. The view from Shining Tor is expansive and can only hope you have a fine day - I did it in early February 1998 in a snowstorm!

WALKING INSTRUCTIONS - Starting from Derbyshire Bridge car park, walk down the road into Goyt's Clough. After more than 1/2 mile turn left, as footpath signed - Stakeside - and follow the path which contours round the valley side and soon you have woodland on your left. In 1/4 mile keep left and walk through the pine trees on the wide track. (Where you turn the path in front is the one from Goytsclough, and if you started from here - 1/4 mile away - you should turn right.) The path curves round to your left in the woodland to some ruins on your left before descending to a footbridge. Follow the ascending path to your right and soon leave the trees as you you walk beside them on your right. Little over 1/4 mile from the footbridge you cross the shallow Stake Clough and continue ascending with a wall on your right. More than 1/4 mile later reach the summit of the moorland, a stile and a track - to your left 3/4 mile away is the Cat & Fiddle Inn!

Turn right keeping the wall on your left and in a few yards turn left over a stile and follow the well defined path, with the wall on your left to the summit of Shining Tor. The actual triangulation pillar is just over the ladder stile. The views are extensive, particularly to Shutlingsloe to your left. The Cheshire Plain unfolds ahead. Just to your west is the site of the Airspeed. The Defiant and Harvard are to the east towards Shooters Cough. Retrace your steps back to the stile and track, 1 /2 mile away. Turn left along the track, with a wall on left; beyond and below is Shooter's Clough. Keep on this descending path for almost a mile to a gate and footpath sign - Errwood Car park. Continue descending slightly right and in 1/4 mile reach a wall and track. If you keep straight ahead you reach the Errwood car park. Turn right along the level track which in more than 1/4 mile gain the one way road in the valley. Cross over and continue on a path, signposted "Riverside Walk". This takes you near the River Goyt before ascending back to the road close to Goytsclough Quarry car park. Turn left and follow the road back to Derbyshire Bridge, little over a mile away. In a few yards on your left is a delightful packhorse bridge over the infant River Goyt.

If you have time available it is worth a side trip - from Errwood Car Park - to see the ruins of Errwood Hall and the surroundings are covered with rhoderdendrons, which in June are a blaze of colour. You can also extend the walk towards Cat's Tor to see the "site" of the two Thunderbolts.

BOULTON PAUL DEFIANT -
POWERED BY ONE 1,030 HP ROLLS ROYCE MERLIN TTI ENGINE.
WING SPAN - 39' 4"
LENGTH - 35' 4"
MAX SPEED - 303 MPH AT 16,500 FT.
ARMAMENTS - 4 .303 BROWNING IN POWER-OP TURRET.

NORTH AMERICAN HARVARD -
2 SEATER TRAINING PLANE.

AIRSPEED OXFORD -
TRAINING PLANE.

REPUBLIC THUNDERBOLT P47C -
USA SINGLE SEATER FIGHTER PLAN - 602 MADE.
1 ENGINE - 2,000 HP R - 2800.21 PRATT & WHITNEY ENGINE.
MAX SPEED - 435 MPH (700 KM)
RANGE - 1,725 MILES (2776 KM)
WEIGHT EMPTY - 10,700 LBS (4858 KG)
WINGSPAN - 40 FT 9" (12.42 M)
LENGTH - 36 FT 1" (10.99M)
HEIGHT - 14FT 7" (4.44M)
ARNAMENTS - 8 - 0.5" MACHINE GUNS ON FRONT WINGS.

North American Harvard FT442 - 5(P)AFU (Advanced Flying Unit)
Crashed 30th November 1944 - Shining Tor
Crew -
Sgt J. Sofranko 788529 (Czech).
The pilot appears to have miscalculated his position and descended in cloud too early hitting the high ground. Killed.

Airspeed Oxford LX745 - 11(P)AFU (Advanced Flying Unit)
Crashed March 12th 1944 - Shining Tor.
Crew -
Fg Off C.S.G. Wood 155765
Plt Off G.C.Liggett J35331 RCAF
Sgt J.G.Hall 133884
They descended through cloud not knowing their position and flew into high ground in bad weather. All killed.

Boulton Paul Defiant T3921 - 96 Sqn.
Crashed October 16th 1941 - Shining Tor.
Crew -
Plt Off M.G.Hilton 66587
Sgtr H.W.Brunckhorst RAAF A404438.
Whilst on a GCI exercise they were flying on instruments unaware they had come out of the cloud. The cloud base was 2,500 ft and the high ground was 2,000ft. At 20.40hrs they flew into high ground; both were injured.

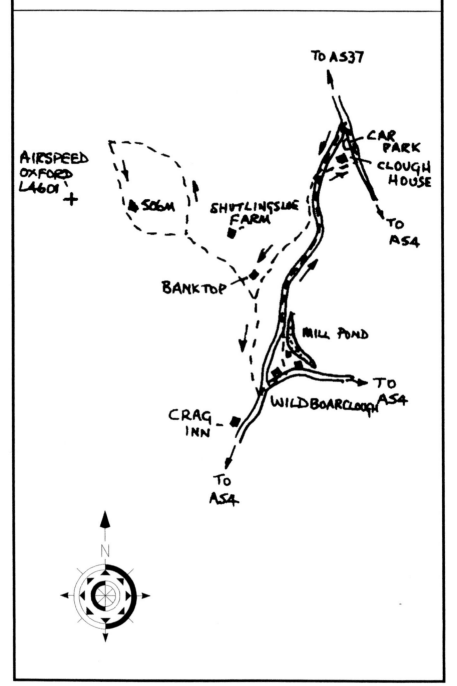

SHUTLINGSLOE
- 4 MILES
- allow 2 hours

Route - *Clough House Car Park - Banktop - Shutlingsloe - Banktop - Wildboarclough - Clough House - Car Park.*

 - 1:25,000 Outdoor Leisure Map - The White Peak - West Sheet.

 - Clough House Car Park. Grid Ref. 988698.

 - Just off the route in Wildboarclough - Crag Inn.

ABOUT THE WALK - An outstanding little walk to the summit of one of true peaks of the Peak District. Close to the summit area and on private land is the site where on April 4th 1945 an Airspeed Oxford L4601 crashed. The walk loops around the summit before descending to Wildboarclough. The hamlet is most attractive where the impressive mill was once the Post Office. The valley was severally flooded on May 24th 1989 and you will see a plaque to this and see several bridges being that date, having been rebuilt. The village also won the 1995 "Best Village" award.

WALKING INSTRUCTIONS - From the car park return to the main road and turn left along it. In less than 1/4 mile, just after passing a pathsign and footbridge on your left to Clough House - your return route - turn right at the pathsign - Langley and Shutlingsloe. The path gently ascends to your left above the road to Banktop House. Pass it on its left side and gain the track. Follow it to a junction and path sign for Shutlingsloe, near a cattle grid. Turn right and ascend the track and where it turns right for Shutlingsloe Farm, bear left as signed with a wall on your right. Ascend to a stile as the ascent becomes more pronounced. The path ahead to the summit is your descent path! Turn right on a mostly level path with a wall to your right. In 1/4 mile reach a ladder stile. Over this the path bears left as you walk through a shallow clough. At the top continue ahead to a wall and the path junction with the summit path to your left and right over the moor to Macclesfield Forest. Turn left and ascend to the summit of Shutlingsloe. On the summit is a plaque to Arthur Smith a footpath fighter. The views from here are extensive and below westwards is the site of the crash. Looking north-east to Shining Tor, is where another Airspeed Oxford came down in 1944. In fact on the eastern side of the tor two other planes came down - a North American Harvard in 1944 and a Boulton Paul Defiant in 1941 - all part of another walk!

From the summit descend steeply down the path you looked up as you ascended the hill. Soon regain your earlier path and retrace it to the track junction. Here turn right along the track and descend to the main road. To your right is the Crag Inn. Turn left then right passing the flood disaster plaque. Ascend past the old mill and before St. Saviour church, turn left, as footpath signed along a track. This leads past the church to a row of cottages. Walk past them - above to your right is mill pond. Descend to the minor road and turn right. Follow the road for more 1/4 mile seeing the bridges and embankments following the 1989 flood. Pass your path to Shutlingsloe and turn right over the footbridge, by the path sign. Follow the path to the righthand side of Clough House. Reaching the farm road turn left back into the car park.

Shutlingsloe.

Airspeed Oxford L4601 - 17 SFTS (Service Flying Training School)
Crashed Shutlingsloe on April 4th 1945.
Crew -
Fg Off K.H.Shawyer 182755 (injured).
Flt Lt H.G.Featonby 128984 (killed)
AC1 G.Fishwick 152868 (killed)
LAC F.Roscoe 1018427 (killed)
Cpl A.J.Burd 978115 (injured).

Flew into high ground in bad weather while on cross country navex The Airspeed Oxford is a training plane.

View from Shutlingsloe to Shining Tor, where another Airspeed Oxford came down.

31

GRADBACH - 6 MILES

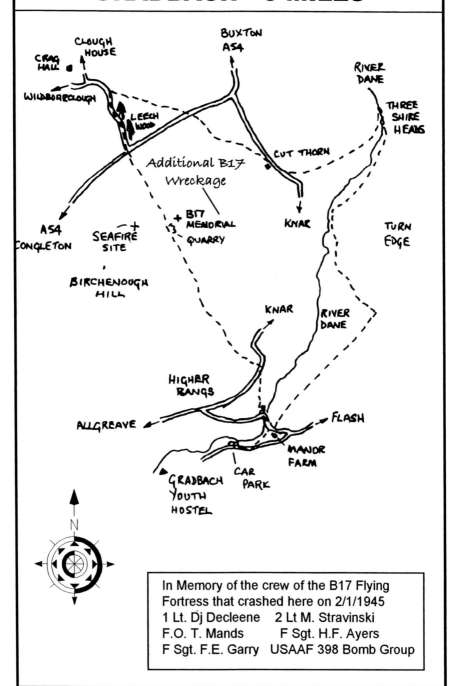

In Memory of the crew of the B17 Flying
Fortress that crashed here on 2/1/1945
1 Lt. Dj Decleene   2 Lt M. Stravinski
F.O. T. Mands   F Sgt. H.F. Ayers
F Sgt. F.E. Garry   USAAF 398 Bomb Group

GRADBACH AND THREE SHIRE HEADS
- 6 MILES
- allow 3 hours.

Route - Gradbach Car park - Higher Bongs - Moorland - A54 - Leech Wood - A54 - Three Shire Heads - Knar - Manor Farm - Gradbach.

 - 1:25,000 Outdoor Leisure Map - The White Peak - West Sheet.

 - Gradbach. Grid Ref. 998664.

 - None.

ABOUT THE WALK - A magnificent walk over moorland to the meeting place of three counties at The Shire Heads - Cheshire, Staffordshire and Derbyshire. Between Gradbach and Wildboarclough is moorland where two Supermarine Seafires came down on July 21st. 1949. The actually site is on private land but the path across here passes the area. Opposite in a small quarry can be seen the monument and small remains of a B17 bomber that came down on the 2nd. January 1945. Views from here are to Shutlingsloe where an Airspeed Oxford came down - see separate walk.

WALKING INSTRUCTIONS - From the car park take the path out of it on its righthand corner - thus avoiding the road. Regain the minor road via a stile and turn left immediately over a footbridge. Keep the River Dane on your left as you cross the field to a stile and pathsign before the road and bridge to your left. Turn left over the bridge and into Cheshire. Pass a chapel and turn right, as footpath signed, by a plaque to Clifford Rathbone - The Stroller - 1907 - 1975. The path ascends to your right above a house and on upto a minor road near Bennettshitch. Cross the road to a gate, pathsign and track. Walk up the walled track to the barn - Higher Bongs. Go through a gate then slightly right to a stile. Bear right to a wall and reach another stile as you gently ascend. Walk onto another then ascend to the skyline to a ladder stile near a small gritstone outcrop. Continue on high ground to another stile and a small quarry. You are now in the area where the Seafire crashed. Above on your right is the B17 monument. Continue ahead on the defined path and soon start descending to the A54 road. Cross over and descend the lane towards Wildboarclough.

In 1/4 mile where the road turns left, turn right, as footpath signed - Three Shire Heads - and walk along the track through Leech Wood to a stile. At first keep a wall on your left before crossing open country, on a defined path, to a stile and the A54 road. Cross over to a stile and path sign - Turn Edge. Follow the defined path across the open field and keep left where the path forks. This leads you gently down to a minor road beneath Cut-Thorn Hill beside a cottage. Turn right then left through a gate and continue descending down a track around the hill leading you down to Three Shire Heads less than 1/2 mile away. Cross the main packhorse bridge and turn right along the track over another bridge. Follow the wide path and where it divides keep right and gently descend with the River Dane to your right. In 1/4 mile keep left as footpath signed and left again at the farm buildings of Knar. Follow the track to a barn on your right and turn right following the track past it. Keep on the track for 1/4 mile to a wall on your right. Continue past it a short distance and turn right - there is no pathsign here. At the end of the field is a ladder stile. Over this the pathline is much clearer with stiles and you basically keep straight ahead with a wall on your right for 1/2 mile. Go through a stile close to a house and turn left to the road at Gradbach. Turn right and in a few yards regain your starting out path and turn left to cross the field to the footbridge and back to the car park.

2004 update - Additional wreckage of the B17 can be seen beyond the monument (GR995677), 200 mtrs. due east at GR997677 - see photograph at end of book.

Supermarine Spitfire -

British made from 1937. Single engine monoplane. The best known single-seat fighter plane of World War 11. Designed by Reginald Mitchell of Hanley, Stoke on Trent. There is a monument to him there. It was the first all metal British fighter and was used by the RAF from 1938 onwards. The engine on the Mk 1A was a Rolls Royce Merlin - more than 1,030 hp - and designed by Arthur Rubbra - a great friend of my late father. The plane saw major action in the Battle of Britain, 1940. The wings were armed with eight .303 Browning machine guns. In 1946 the Mk24 was brought into service together with a Seafire, for use from aircraft carriers.

Max speed - 367 m.p.h. (591km).
Wingspan - 36' 10" (11.3m).
Length - 29' 11' (9.1m).
Ceiling height - 37,000 ft.
Rate of climb - 2,666 ft per minute.
Range - 470 miles
Weight - 7,500 lbs.

B17 Flying Fortress Monument - August 2004

BOEING B – 17G Flying Fortress. –
USA – 10 Crew heavy bomber.
Engine – 4 – 1,200hp Wright R–1820 – 97 nine cylinder radial engines.
Max speed – 302mph (486km)
Range – 1,800 miles (2,897km)
Weight – empty – 44,560lbs (20,212kg)
       Max – 72,000lbs (32,659kg)
Wingspan – 103ft 0" (31.63m)
Length – 74ft 9" (22.78m)
Height – 19ft 1" (5.82m)
Arnaments – 13 overall – 2 –0.5" machine guns Chin turret
 – 1 – 0.5" machine gun in each check position,
2 – 0.5" machine gun Dorsal turret.
 – 1 – 0.5" machine guns in roof position.
 – 2 – 0.5" machine guns Ventral position
– 2 – 0.5" machine guns tail

35

THE ROACHES - 5 MILES

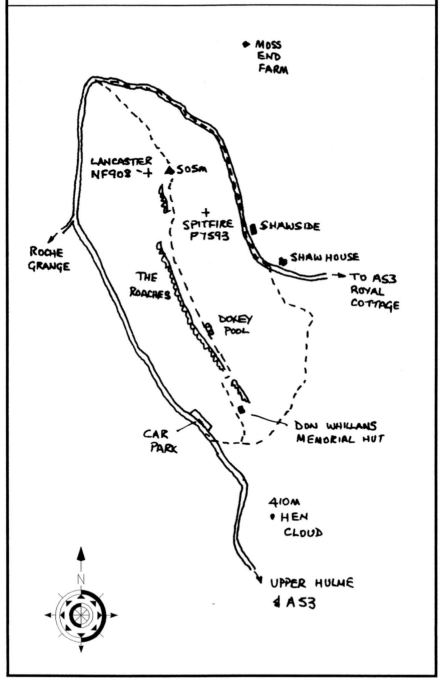

MOSS END FARM

LANCASTER NF908

505m

SPITFIRE P7593

SHAWSIDE

SHAW HOUSE

TO A53 ROYAL COTTAGE

ROCHE GRANGE

THE ROACHES

DOXEY POOL

DON WHILLANS MEMORIAL HUT

CAR PARK

410M HEN CLOUD

UPPER HULME & A53

N

THE ROACHES
- 5 MILES
- allow 2 to 3 hours.

Route - The Roaches - Doxey Pool - Trig Point 505m. - Bearstone Rock - Lane - Shaw House - The Roaches.

 - 1:25,000 Outdoor Leisure Map - The White Peak - West Sheet.

 - Beneath The Roaches. Grid Ref. 004622.

 - None. Nearest The Rock Inn, Upper Hulme.

 - Roaches Tea Room.

ABOUT THE WALK - The Roaches has always been a place of fascination and where wallabies were once seen. This walk takes along the spine of the rocks and near the highest point on the eastern side a Supermarine Spitfire No. P7593 crashed on 17th November 1940. On the western side a Avro Lancaster No. NF908, crashed on the 3rd. January 1945. Being open country you can explore the sites. There is nothing to be seen at the Spitfire site and of the Lancaster site apart from two hollows, there is likewise nothing to be seen.Also in the area a German Junkers Bomber came down at Moss End Farm. At Hen Cloud a Weelington bomber came down.

WALKING INSTRUCTIONS - From the car park turn left through the gate and ascend the track towards The Roaches. After a short distance turn left onto a path and soon pass Rockhall - the Don Whillans Memorial Hut - and just past it turn right and ascend to the right of a gritstone buttress and ascend steps to the top. Here turn left and on your left is a stone seat and memorial to the prince and Princess of Teck - August 23rd. 1872. Continue on the path past the highest rock face of the Roaches and approaching a fence turn right and ascend to the top. Here turn left with a wall on your left and walk along the spine of The Roaches. In 1/4 mile pass Doxey Pool on your right. Little over 1/4 mile later pass a concessionary path on your right and less than five minutes later the path bears right to begin the final ascent to the triangulation pillar. Here to your right is where the Spitfire came down and to your left near the rocks is where the Lancaster crashed.

Continue onto the trig point and descend the path beyond, on stone slabs and pass Bearstone Rock before gaining the road. The views ahead are worth noting - northwards is moorland above Wildboarclough where a Supermarine Seafire came down. Beyond is the prominent shape of Shutlingsloe where an Airspeed Oxford came down. Both are separate walks for you to do!.

Turn right along the road and ascend at first then descend the road for a mile, passing the other end of the concessionary path and reaching Shaw House on your left turn right, as footpath signed, along a track towards Shawtop. Nearing the house the path has been diverted; turn left and follow the stiles around the lefthand side of the house. Follow the stiled path to a track. Turn right along it and in 200 yards, where it turns left for Summerhill, keep ahead to agate and follow the path beyond beside the field boundary on your left. This soon brings over the crest with views to Hen Cloud. The path soon becomes a track as you pick up your start out route and regain the road and car park.

Avro Lancaster NF908 - 96 Sqd
Crashed The Roaches at 1600hrs on January 3rd. 1945
Crew -
Pilot - Plt Off W.V.W. Allamby RAAF A428516 (Royal Austrailian Air Force)
Bomb Aimer - Flt Sgt G.J.Dunbar RAAF A424391
W/Operator - Flt Sgt R.Emonson RAAF A430484
F/Engineer - Sgt N. Lees 2218806 RAFVR
Navigator - Flt Lt J.I. Pritchard RAAF A421047
Air Gunner - Flt Sgt T.E.H.Wright RAAF A430728
Rear Gunner - Flt Sgt C.C.Watson RAAF A434547
Whilst on a fighter affiliation and naviagtion exercise they descended to get a visual fix on their position. They hit just below the summit of the Roaches with wreckage strewn over a wide area. All killed.

Supermarine Spitfire P7593 - 4FPP (Ferry Pilot's Pool)
Crashed The Roaches late Sunday morning on November 17th 1940
Crew -
Sgt J.B.White - killed on impact *
Flew into high ground whilst ferrying the new plane from Kirkbride to West Malling. A wing caught the top of the Roaches and ripped off. The plane hit marshy ground 600 feet away. The nose section was buried 10ft deep. The engine was recovered in 1975 by the Derby Historical Aviation Society.

November 2004 update. In Meersbrook churchyard I met an elderley man who worked for the Brocklehurst family at Swythamley Hall. He recalled seeing the Junkers on fire. He also delivered milk to Benthead Farm, beneath the Roaches, where one morning he saw an engine that had fallen off a Spitfire. He also informed me of another plane that crashed beneath The Mermaid Inn.

Hen Cloud - A Wellington bomber no. Z1744 came down at GR SK008614 on November 11th. 1944.

Junkers 88 Bomber came down at Moss End Farm, (Quarnford) GR SK004648 on 8th. May 1941. The bomber had come from an airfield in northern France to bomb the northern cities and hit the countryside and all four crew were killed. The RAF removed the wreckage and the bodies were given a funeral by the Vicar of St. Edward the Confessor, Leek. They were interred in Leek cemetry in graves purchased by the War Graves Commission. There are no memorials; only the coffins remain as the bodies were exhumed. the crew were -

Pilot - Flight Lieutenant (Hauptmann) Dietrich Heistermann Von - Zichelberg; aged 31. The word Von means he was a titled (aristocrat).

Navigator/Bomb-aimer - Flying Officer (Oberleutnant) W. Leemke. ID Disc BIA 71042-8. Age not known.

Wireless Operator/Air Gunner - Flight Sergeant (Oberfeld Webel) Rudolf Schwalbe. Aged 24.

Engineer/Air Gunner - Sergeant (Feldwebel) G.Mahl. Age not known.

There is a very gruesome account by Ernest Bowyer, who was in the Home Guard, and was one of the first on the scene. He was to see *"Nothing worse when I was in the army"*. Together with an RAF Officer from Chester they searched the wreckage and only after a long while found the fourth body; they were standing on it! The Officer removed his Iron Cross, Luger pistol and a bunch of keys.

THE JUNKERS BOMBER WAS GERMANY'S MOST SUCCESSFUL BOMBER - MORE THAN 7,000 WERE MADE.
ENGINES - 2 - 1340 HP JUNKERS JUMO 211J-1/2 12 CYLINDER
MAX SPEED - 292 M.P.H.
CEILING - 26,900 FT. (8,200M)
RANGE - 1,696 MILES (2,730 KM.)
WINGSPAN - 65FT. 7INS. LENGTH - 47 FT. 3INS. HEIGHT - 16FT.
BOMBLOAD - 5,511 LBS. (2,500 KG).

The only other "crash" in the area was when a German plane discarded its last remaining bomb on its way home. It fell and killed a cow! Another stray bomb fell in the next parish and demolished Earl Sterndale church; after the war the church was rebuilt.

GRINDON MOOR - 7 MILES

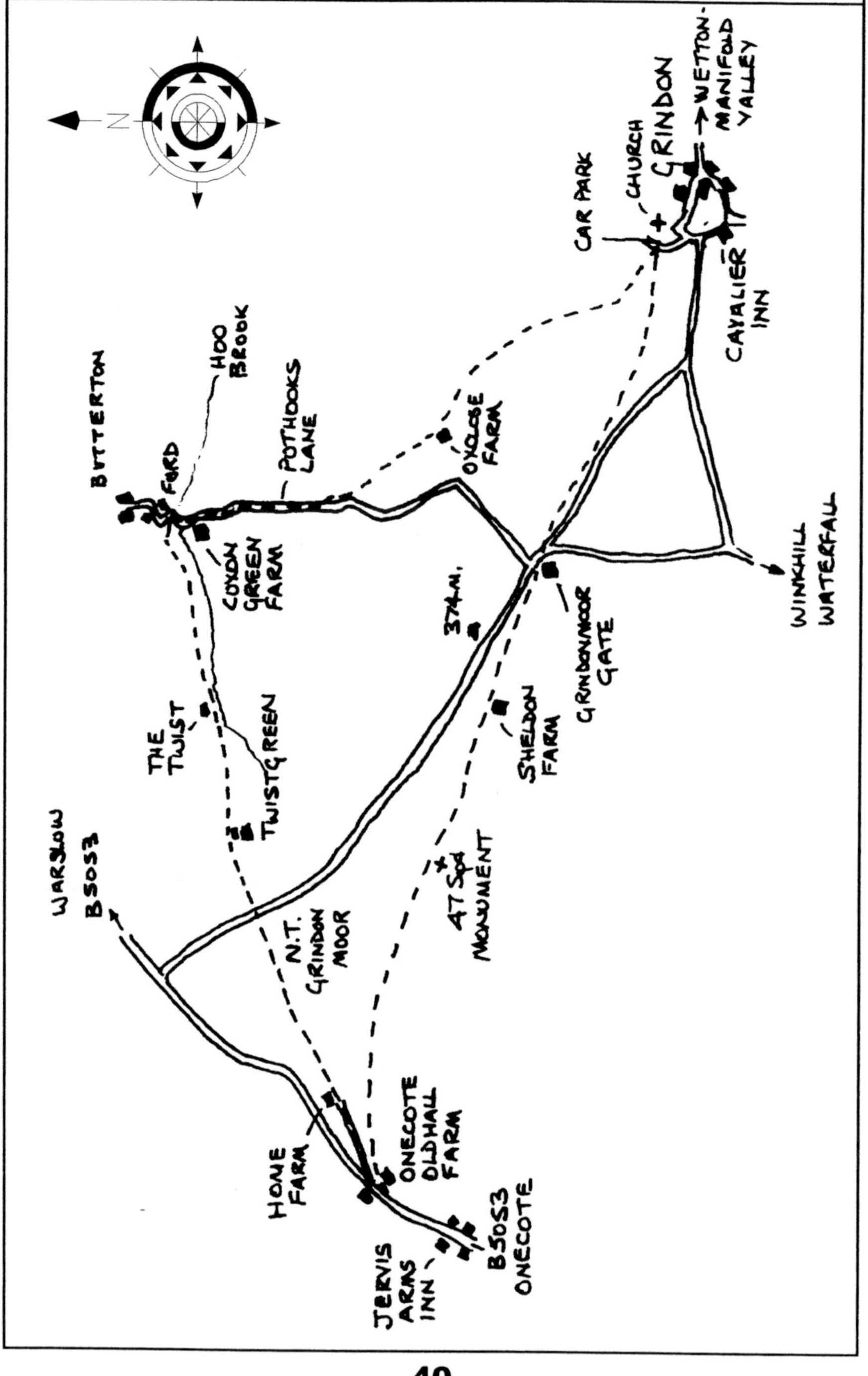

GRINDON MOOR
- 7 MILES
- allow 3 hours.

Route - Grindon - Grindon Moor Gate - 47 Sqd. Memorial Cairn - Onecote Old Hall Farm - Grindon Moor (National Trust) - Twistgreen - Butterton - Pothooks Lane - Oxclose Farm - Grindon.

Map - 1:25,000 Outdoor Leisure Map No. 24 - The White Peak - West sheet.

Car Park and start - Just north of the church; park and picnic tables. GR SK085646.

Inns - The Cavalier Inn, Grindon. Jervis Arms, Onecote. The Black Horse Inn, Butterton - all just off the route!

ABOUT THE WALK - The aim is quite simply to walk across high ground with stunning views to the Manifold Valley and westwards over the Staffordshire Moorlands, to the 47 Sqd. Memorial Cairn. This marks close to the spot where a Halifax bomber, crashed on the 13th. February 1947 killing all the crew and press photographers, whilst on a mercy mission to drop supplies to the surrounding villages, because of the severe winter. I came here on Remembrance Day and experienced wild conditions of low cloud, mist and strong wind. I stood alone at the cairn. I first came here on a summers day and was amazed at the views and realised had the plane been twenty feet higher would have cleared the moor; but the conditions dictated otherwise. You descend to the outskirts of Onecote, before crossing the moorland and descending to the ford at Butterton. One final gentle ascent returns you to Grindon.

WALKING INSTRUCTIONS - There is a Grindon historical plaque on the lefthand side of the car park. From the car park area head for the righthand side exit with two stiles and paths opposite. The one on the right is your return path. Take the one on the left, with the picnic tables and pond well to your left. The path line is not defined at first. Walk westwards across the middle of the field to the lefthand end of a wall - to your right is woodland - there is no stile here. Bear slightly right and cross the next field to a wooden stile. Continue with a fence to your right and Grindon Road to your left. You now keep in the fields with the road on your left for 1/4 mile to near a road junction and stiles.

41

Cross the road, at Grindonmoor Gate, to a stile and path sign and onto another and walk past a house on your right to a stile. Follow a small embankment across the field and pass the end of two stone walls on your left. Keep ahead to a stone stile in a wall on your left. Cross the field beyond to a stile and path sign at Sheldon Farm. Walk around the metal building, as signed, to a stile and basically keep straight ahead across the field to a stile and onto another. Keep to the righthand side of the field to a stile on your right. Over this turn left along the lefthand side of the field to another stile and onto the 47 Sqd. Memorial Cairn.

Continue along the lefthand side of the field to a stile. Keep ahead and soon cross a track and bear slightly right across the field to a stile in a dip. Descend the righthand side of the field, passing a farm building on your right. Further down go through a gate and continue descending with a large ditch on your right. Further right is Home Farm which you be walking past shortly. Reaching Onecote Old Hall Farm, go over a stile by a path sign and descend to your left to a stile at the start of the farm drive off the B5053 road. 100 yards to your left along the road is the Jervis Arms. Turn right along the road for a few yards to the tarmaced drive to Home Farm on your right. Walk up the road passing the farm on your left, where it now becomes a track. Where the track turns sharp right, ahead to your left is a stile and path sign. Go over and continue ascending, at first following a line of electric poles, and soon keep a wall on your left with ruined farm beyond. Reach a stile and gain Grindon Moor - National Trust property. The path becomes more defined as you cross a heather moorland to the Grindon Road.

Go straight across to a stile and continue on a track, which soon bears right to Twistgreen. You keep straight ahead to a stile on the left of the buildings. Cross to a gate on your left and continue descending near the righthand side of the field and pass another ruined farm on your right. Continue to a stile and onto another close to the house, The Twist. Walk past it on your right above a stream - Hoo Brook - to a stile. Continue ahead across ten well stiled fields as you head towards Butterton. Nearing the village turn right down a walled path to emerge close the village's ford. Turn right along the Grindon Road - Pothooks Lane - and cross another ford via a footbridge on your right. Ascend the lane passing Coxton Green Farm on your right. 1/4 mile later and before the lane turns right, on your left is a stile. Go through and turn right, first keeping the lane over the hedge on your right. Where it turns right bear slightly left to a stile. Keep to the righthand side of the field to three more stiles before Oxclose Farm. Walk through to your left and keep to the high ground to a hedge on your right - the spire of Grindon church acts as your guide. To your left are views to the Manifold Valley and Thor's Cave. Keep the hedge on your right to stiles eventually reaching a stile before the car park. Cross the road back into it.

47 Sqd. Memorial Cairn - At GR 063553 is a memorial to the sad crash of a Halifax bomber No. RT 922 F, that crashed on 13th. February 1947. The plane was on a Food Relief Mission to drop supplies to the snow bound villages, because of the record breaking blizzard, in the Staffordshire Moorlands. All six crew were killed together with two press reporters. With the area cut off and on limited electrical supply it was decided to drop supplies. A reconnaissance plane came over from Fairford, Gloucestershire, and reported back of heavy icing on the wings. The next day a Halifax flew over very low with its bomb doors open but moments later crashed. The Rector of Grindon, Canon Cowen, phoned Fairfield and pleaded that no more planes were sent to avoid further loss of life. The dead were buried in Buxton.

The six crew -

Pilot - Sqdn Leader Donald McIntyre (33269) from Gloucestershire. Aged 31.

Navigator - Flight Lieutenant Ernest Smith (164809) from Nottinghamshire. Aged 23.

Wireless Operator - Sig 11 Flight Sergeant Kenneth Charles Pettit (1876996) from Surrey. Aged 21.

Flight Engineer - Eng. Warrant Officer Richard Sydney Kearns (3930875) from Kingsbury, Middlesex. Aged 22.

Ground Crew - Warrant Officer Gordon Victor Chapman, from Dagenham. Aged 24.

Second Pilot - Sergeant William Sherry of the Glider Pilot Regiment from Burslem, Staffs. Aged 24

Two civilians - Press photographers - both from London -

Joseph John Reardon, aged 32, for the Keystone Press Agency.

David William Saville, aged 33, for the Daily Herald.

13. HANDLEY PAGE HALIFAX -
A MAJOR RAF HEAVY SEVEN SEAT BOMBER DURING THE SECOND PART OF WWLL. COST ABOUT £50,000 IN 1943

4-1,615 HP - BINNLOT HERCULES VI ENGINES.

MAX SPEED - 282 MPH (454 KM)

RANGE - 1,985 MILES - (3,194 KM) WITH 7,000LB (3,175 KG) BOMB LOAD. (INTERNAL BOMB LAOD 14,700 LBS - (6,577 KG)

WEIGHT EMPTY - 42,500 LBS - (19,278 KG) MAX - 65,000 LBS - (29,484 KG).

WINGSPAN - 98FT 8" - (30.07M)

LENGTH - 71FT 4"- (21.74M)

HEIGHT - 20FT 1" - (6.12M)

ARNAMENTS - NOSE TURRET - 1 - 0.303 MACHINE GUN. DORSAL TURRET - 4 - 0.303 MACHINE GUN.

47 SQD. Monument.

WESTON UNDERWOOD -5 MILES

WESTON UNDERWOOD
- 5 MILES
- allow 2 hours.

Route - Weston Underwood - Burland Green Lane - Monument - Burland Green Lane - Moseyley - Gun Hills - Woodfall Lane - Draycott Plantation - Weston Underwood.

 - 1:25,000 Explorer Series No.259 - Derby.

 - None, roadside only.

 - None. Nearest north of Weston Underwood - The Cock Inn.

ABOUT THE WALK - I had not expected to learn of a memorial to an aircrew so far south. I was told about it quite by chance and the day before planning to walk the area and search for it, someone called in to see me and said she had walked past it, yesterday! The walk takes you across the fields to a monument to the crew of a Whitley Bomber that crashed here on July 24th 1944, some eight miles short of their destination, Ashbourne airfield. The walk takes around high ground and on my walk I would have thought I was in moorland with curlews calling, skylarks singing above, and startled grouse darting away in front of me. It is a delightful walk with good views to Duffield.

WALKING INSTRUCTIONS - The walk commences from the southern end of Weston Underwood, at the junction of Bullhurst Lane, Cutler Lane and Burland Green Lane. Walk along Burland Green Lane, opposite Cutler Lane and Inn Farm, and just past Pennine Lodge on your left, turn left at the gate and and footpath sign. In a few yards turn left along the field edge and descend to a footbridge. Cross this and ascend slightly to your right to a stile. Continue across the next field to a stile and then keep the fence on your right, which later becomes a hedge, as you pass a disused pit on your left. In the latter stages you have the embankment on your left. Just after go through a gap by a solitary tree, with yellow arrow, and keep beside the hedge on your left to walk around the field to a stile. Cross the next field to a stile and through this you can see

47

the monument ahead to your right. After looking at the monument, ahead can be seen a gate and yellow arrow. Go through the gate and keep beside the hedge on your left - you are walking along the approach of the plane - to a stile. Continue ahead beside the hedge and soon descend to a gate and Burland Green Lane.

Turn right and in a few yards left, at the footpath sign and gate. Descend along the hedgeside to a gate and onto Moseyley Farm. Walk through the farmyard to the lane. Cross over to a stile and path sign and you destination is the lefthand side of the prominent pine plantation on Gun Hill. Cross the field slightly to your right to a stile, then keep the hedge on your left as you ascend to a stile and towards the wood. At the end of the field descend to your left to a stile and down to another to Gunhills Lane beside Gunhills Farm on your left. Turn right along the lane around the hill to the second footpath sign on your left. Go through the stile and cross diagonally right across the field past the end of hedge and onto a stile and path sign beside Woodfall Lane.

Turn left along the lane and after 50 yards turn right at a stile and pathsign. The pathline is faint but angles left over the brow of the field and once there you can see the stile ahead. Your pathline is to the right of the house - Newlands - to the corner of a hedge track ahead. Basically following the same direction cross the field to the next stile and onto another before gaining the corner of the hedged track. Gaining the track turn right to a gate and descend the field to a footbridge. Ascend the next field aiming for the top lefthand corner, where on the left of three trees is the stile. Keep the hedge on your right to the next stile, then cross a field to another stile followed by a small gate with Draycott Plantation (pine) to your right. Continue ahead to a stile and footbridge and down to another. Ascend the field beyond bearing slightly left to a stile at the top. Through gain a track and descend this to a stile and pathsign and Burland Green Lane. Turn left and in a few strides pass your earlier path and reach the crossroads in Weston Underwood.

Monument -

This stone was laid
to mark the last resting place,
whilst on Active Service, of -
Flt Sgt (Pilot) J.W.E. Cooper - aged 24
Sgt (Navigator) H.Cowan - aged 21
Sgt (Wireless Operator) W.C.Norcross - aged 21
Also in memory of
Sgt (Bomb Aimer) W.B. Smith - aged 21
interred Ashbourne
and
Sgt (Air Gunner) M.M. Lyon - aged 18
interred St. Helens.
who gave their lives in
comradeship on July 24th 1944.

The Whitley Bomber was heading for Ashbourne Airfield, 8 miles away. The crew were on a training mission having collected the aircraft following repair. An engine caught fire and the pilot, Flt Sgt Cooper, managed to avoid Weston Underwood and crashed into the high ground above, creating a 19ft. crater as it nose dived. The locals rushed to help but there were no survivors. Three of the bodies were never recovered and one was found two days later having been thrown upon impact. On remembrance day a service takes place at the memorial.

The Post Mistress of Weston Underwood, Mrs Harriet Yates, and her sister in law watched the bomber pass from their window.
" We could see it coming down and it was on fire. We did not know then it was one of ours and we did not hear until the following day about the crash."

The Armstrong Whitworth Whitley Bomber had two Merlin engines and was tested at Hucknall, Nottinghamshire. The first squadron to be equipped with the plane was the 10 Sqd at Dishforth, Yorkshire. Built in Bagington, Coventry. By July 1943 1,824 had been built.

DAM BUSTERS WALK - 10 MILES

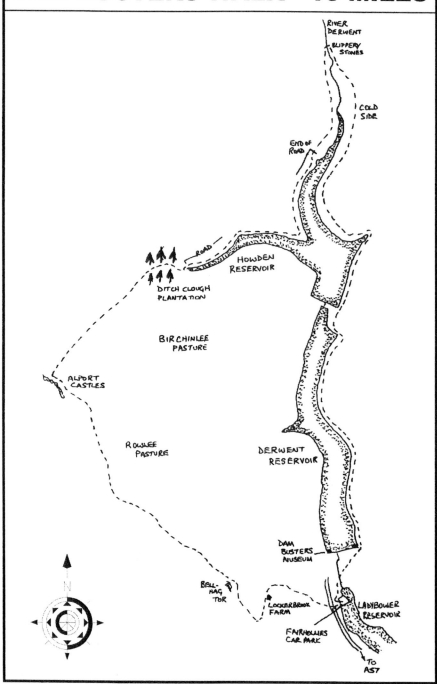

RIVER DERWENT

SLIPPERY STONES

COLD SIDE

END OF ROAD

ROAD

HOWDEN RESERVOIR

DITCH CLOUGH PLANTATION

BIRCHINLEE PASTURE

ALPORT CASTLES

ROWLEE PASTURE

DERWENT RESERVOIR

DAM BUSTERS MUSEUM

BELL-HAG TOR

LOCKERBROOK FARM

FAIRHOLMES CAR PARK

LADYBOWER RESERVOIR

TO A57

N

DAM BUSTERS WALK ALPORT CASTLES AND DERWENT RESERVOIR - 10 MILES - allow 3 1/2 to 4 hours.

ROUTE - Fairholmes Car Park - Lockerbrook Coppice - Lockerbrook Farm - Bellhag Tor - Rowlee Pasture - Alport Castles - Birchinlee Pasture - Ditch Clough Plantation - Howden Reservoir - King's Tree - Slippery Stones - Cold Side - Cal-Der-Went Walk - Derwent Reservoir - Fairholmes Car Park.

 - 1:25,000 Outdoor Leisure Map - The Dark Peak.

 - Fairholmes, Derwent Valley. Grid Ref. SK173893.

 - limited Refreshments at Fairholmes Car Park.

ABOUT THE WALK - One of my earliest recollections of a "hard" winter walk in the Peak District, was around this area and onto Alport Castles. As I recall it was a wild day, cold and snowing hard, but me and my companion had just crossed Kinder, using ice-axes and crampons in Fair Brook Naze. After a couple of hours we neared Alport Castles and climbed the rocky summit of The Tower, where we sheltered by a boulder and ate a chocolate bar. This was an early "summit" for both of us and the ascent brought a rich glow to our numbed senses. The feeling of adventure that day, has never died, and this walk to Alport Castles, has become something of a pilgrimage over the years. I did this walk again in mid October 1996, in perfect conditions, wearing just a T shirt and shorts. The views over Alport and Derwent Valleys were a joy to behold. As I descended to Derwent Reservoir, the autumn colours of the forest glowed brilliantly in the warm sun. The west tower of Derwent Reservoir has a Dambusters Museum.

Although not a walk to an aircraft crash site, I have included this walk as part of the aircraft theme. The valley is rich in modern history, with the "lost" village of Derwent beneath Ladybower Reservoir. The reservoir filled valley was a training ground for the famous Dam Buster raid and by a sheer quirk of fate, Sir Barnes Wallis, (the creator of the bouncing bomb) was born just a few doors away from where I am writing this in Ripley. The walk is longer than usual but after the initial ascent it is all down hill! There are also a couple of options, missing out Alport Castles. You can just walk around just Derwent and Howden Reservoirs - about 5 miles. Or, during the season take the bus to the end of the valley and walk back down the eastern side - about 3 miles.

WALKING INSTRUCTIONS - From the car park, follow the road out back to the valley road. Cross over to your left to the Concessionary Path to Lockerbrook. Ascend the wide path through Lockerbrook Coppice to a forest track. Here turn left along it, following round to your right to a sign - Forest Path. Turn left and follow this through the pine trees to the private path to Lockerbrook Farm. Turn right and ascend to a stile on the forest edge. Ascend the field to a stile and track. Turn left and ascend the track past Lockerbrook Farm and onto the track summit and junction 1/4 mile away. Turn right and ascend the path to ladder stile. Continue near a wall on your left to a stile and boundary of Open Country. You now enter National Trust property - Rowlee Estate. Continue on a well defined path across the moorland to Alport Castles, 1 1/2 miles away.

When almost level with The Tower, turn right , with a wall on your left and descend the wide path past Grouse shooting butts - now in National Trust property - Birchenlee Pasture. Reach a gate and enter Ditch Clough Plantation. For the remainder of the walk - 5 miles - you are in forest. Descend the track and at the bottom turn right to the valley road. Turn left along it passing through Banktop Plantation and Nether Wood Plantation. On your right is Howden Reservoir and you will soon be walking down the other side! At the end of the road, continue on the track still in woodland to the packhorse bridge at Slippery Stones.

Cross the bridge and bear right and ascend the path to a track. Turn right along it and at first walk above the trees with views of valley, as you walk round Cold Side. After 1/2 mile you are back into the trees as you walk through Ronksley Wood. You are now following the "Cal-Der-Went Walk", a magnificent 35 mile walk from the River Calder to the end of Ladybower Reservoir - hence its name. Continue past the dam wall of Howden Reservoir and continue beside Derwent Reservoir. In less than 2 miles you approach the towers of Derwent Reservoir wall. Go through a stile on your right and in a few yards right again and descend overlooking the wall to a road. Bear right and in a few yards leave it on your left to follow the path back to the car park.

It is worth visiting the Ladybower Inn on the A57 to see the inn sign recording the the 617 squadron who carried out the daring raid in Germany.

The Dam Busters Raid
The Squadron was formed at Scampton on March 21st 1943, with Guy Gibson the Squadron Leader. He was allowed to choose his own men for the mission. Twenty-three Avro Lancaster Bombers were converted to carry Barnes Wallis "bouncing bomb." The bomb, which was a cylindrical container filled with 6,600 lbs of explosives had to be dropped exactly at -
- a height of 60 feet.
- at a speed of 220 mph.

The destination was the Ruhr with three dams - Mohre, Eder and Sorpe, which combined contained 300 million gallons of water, for the Reich's arms industry. The raid took place on May 16th 1943 with nineteen aircraft. Five were shot down before reaching the Ruhr. Guy Gibson lead the attack just after midnight with an attack on the Mohre Dam, which was breached. Three aircraft attacked the Eder Dam and this was breached. Attacks on the Sorpe Dam failed, but despite this the raid was a major success. Guy Gibson received the V.C.

Barnes Neville Wallis
Was born in Ripley, Derbyshire in 1887. (died 1979) Among his many achievements he designed the airship R100 and the Swallow variable sweep wing principal. This allowed the sweep of a wing to be changed in flight enabling an aircraft to fly supersonic and also at low speeds. In the 1930's he invented the geodetic form of aircraft construction which was used to build the Wellington bomber. His most famous work was the "bouncing bomb" or "shock wave" mine used in the Dam Busters raid. He was knighted in 1968.

Some brief notes about the planes -

THE VICKERS WELLINGTON BOMBER-
BRITISH MADE AND DATES FROM 1940 AND USED AS A LONG RANGE BOMBER, PRIMARILY ON NIGHT
RAIDS.
POWERED BY TWO 1,000 HP BRITISH PEGASUS XVIII ENGINES.
MAX SPEED - 235M.P.H. (378KM). AT 15,500 FT.
RATE OF CLIMB - 1,120 FEET PER MINUTE.
CEILING HEIGHT - 18,000 FEET.
RANGE - 1,200 MILES.
WINGSPAN - 86' 2" (26.3M.)
LENGTH - 64' 7" (19.7M.)

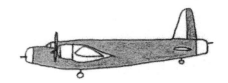

ARMAMENTS -
NOSE TURRET - 2 .303 MACHINE GUNS
TAIL TURRET - 2 .303 MACHINE GUNS.

AVRO LANCASTER -
ORIGINALLY DESIGNED AS THE AVRO MANCHESTER 111 IN 1939 BUT WAS SOON RENAMED THE
LANCASTER AND PRIMARILY USED AS NIGHT BOMBER.
POWERED BY FOUR ENGINES MERLIN 1,460 HP.
MAX SPEED - 275 M.P.H. AT 15,000 FT (FULLY LOADED)
CRUISING SPEED - 200 MPH AT 15,000 FT.
- 245 MPH AT SEA ;LEVEL.
RANGE - 2,530 MILES (7,000 LB LOAD)
- 1,730 MILES (12,000 LB LOAD)
- 1,550 MILES (22,000 LB LOAD)
SERVICE CEILING HEIGHT - 19,000 FT.
ARMAMENTS -
- NOSE TURRET - 2 .303 MACHINE GUNS.
- TAIL TURRET - 4 .303 MACHINE GUNS.

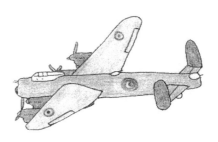

WINGSPAN - 102' (31.1M.)
LENGTH - 69' 6" (21.2M)
WEIGHT - 65,000 LBS
BOMB LOAD - INITIALLY 8,000 LBS BUT MODIFIED TO 22,000 LBS.
CREW - 7

THE LANCASTER SERVED FROM JANUARY 1942 IN 54 SQUADRONS. BETWEEN THEM THEY DROPPED
OVER 60% OF BOMBER COMMAND TONNAGE THROUGHPUT THE WAR. NEARLY 4,000 WERE LOST,
MAINLY IN ACTION. OUT OF A TOTAL OF 32 V.C.'S AWARDED NINE WERE PRESENTED TO LANCASTER
CREWS.

SUPERMARINE SPITFIRE -
BRITISH MADE FROM 1937. SINGLE ENGINE MONOPLANE. THE BEST KNOWN SINGLE-SEAT FIGHTER
PLANE OF WORLD WAR 11. DESIGNED BY REGINALD MITCHELL OF HANLEY, STOKE ON TRENT. THERE IS
A MONUMENT TO HIM THERE. IT WAS THE FIRST ALL METAL BRITISH FIGHTER AND WAS USED BY THE
RAF FROM 1938 ONWARDS. THE ENGINE ON THE MK 1A WAS A ROLLS ROYCE MERLIN - MORE THAN 1,030
HP - AND DESIGNED BY ARTHUR RUBBRA - A GREAT FRIEND OF MY LATE FATHER. THE PLANE SAW MAJOR
ACTION IN THE BATTLE OF BRITAIN, 1940. THE WINGS WERE ARMED WITH EIGHT .303 BROWNING
MACHINE GUNS. IN 1946 THE MK24 WAS BROUGHT INTO SERVICE TOGETHER WITH A SEAFIRE, FOR USE
FROM AIRCRAFT CARRIERS.
MAX SPEED - 367 M.P.H. (591KM).
WINGSPAN - 36' 10" (11.3M)
LENGTH - 29' 11" (9.1M).
CEILING HEIGHT - 37,000 FT.
RATE OF CLIMB - 2,666 FT PER MINUTE.
RANGE - 470 MILES
WEIGHT - 7,500 LBS.

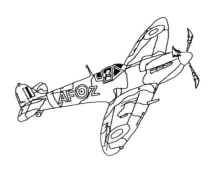

BOULTON PAUL DEFIANT
POWERED BY ONE 1,030 HP ROLLS ROYCE MERLIN 111 ENGINE.
WING SPAN - 39' 4"
LENGTH - 35' 4"
MAX SPEED - 303 MPH AT 16,500 FT.
ARMAMENTS - 4 .303 BROWNING IN POWER-OP TURRET.

DE HAVILLAND VAMPIRE-
POWERED BY ONE 3,000LB D.H.GOBLIN ENGINE.
WING SPAN - 40'
LENGTH - 30' 9"
MAX SPEED - 540 MPH AT 20,000 FEET.
RATE OF CLIMB - 4,200 FEET ME MINUTE.
RANGE - 730 MILES
ARMAMENTS - 4 X 30MM FUSELAGE NOSE.

AIRSPEED OXFORD -
THREE-SEAT ADVANCED TRAINER. WOODEN STRUCTURE, PLYWOOD- COVERED. THE RAF'S FIRST TWIN
ENGINED MONOPLANE TRAINER. STARTED IN USE IN NOVEMBER 1937; OVER 8,700 BUILT.
MAKER'S DESIGNATION - AS10 (OXFORD I AND II); AS46 (OXFORD V).
MANUFACTURERS - AIRSPEED (1934) LTD, PORTSMOUTH AND CHRISTCHURCH. SUB-CONTRACTED
BY D.H.,STNDARD AND PERCIVAL.
ENGINE - MK II: TWO 370HP ARMSTRONG SIDDELEY CHEETAH X.
- MK V: TWO 450HP PRATT & WHITNEY WASP JUNIOR.
DIMENSIONS - SPAN, 53FT 4IN; LENGTH, 34FT 6IN; HEIGHT 11FT 1 IN; WING AREA, 348SQ FT.
WEIGHTS - MK II: EMPTY, 5,380LB; LOADED, 7,600LB. MK V: EMPTY, 5670LB; LOADED, 8,000LB.
PERFORMANCE - MK II: MAX SPEED,188MPH; CLIMB, 960FT / MIN; SERVICE CEILING, 19,500FT. MK
V: MAX SPEED, 202 MPH; CLIMB, 2,000FT/MIN; SERVICE CEILING, 21,000FT.

NORTH AMERICAN AT-6 HARVARD (TEXAN)
COUNTRY OF ORIGIN   -   USA. CHEAP TRAINER PLANE WITH HANDLING CHARACTERISTICS OF A
FIGHTER PLANE. ABOUT 15,000 WERE BUILT. FIRST FLIGHT IN APRIL 1936 AND USED UNTIL 1955.

ENGINES - PRATT & WHITNEY R-1340-49 WASP 9- CYLINDER RADIAL, AIR COOLED, 600 HP.
CREW - TWO
MAX SPEED - 208MPH (335 KM/H)
RANGE - 750 MILES (1,025 KM)
CEILING - 24,200FT (7,325M)
LENGTH - 29FT 0IN (8.84M)
SPAN - 42FT 0IN (12.80M)
HEIGHT - 11FT 9IN (3.55M)

The Miles Magister - was a monoplane largely built of wood.

The Gipsy Moth - Biplane with two crew. The engine had a speed upto 135 m.p.h. and had a cruising speed of 120 m.p.h. It had a low landing speed of only 70 m.p.h.

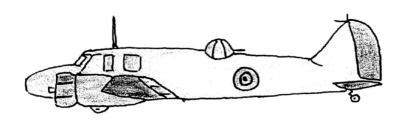

AVRO ANSON Mk 1 (N9912) -
UK built from 1934 - 1952. Primarily as a light transport or coastal reconnaissance plane. Known as the "faithful Annie". More than 11,000 were built.
Engine - two 355 hp Armstrong Siddeley Cheetah 1X
Max. speed - 188 mph (302.5 km)
Ceiling - 19,000 ft. (5,790m)
Range - 1,271 km.
Weight - Empty - 5375 lbs (2,438 kg)
Armaments - Max. of 4 - 0.303 machine gun.
Dimension - Wingspan - 56'-6" (17.22m)
Length - 42 ft 3in (12.88 m)
Height - 3.99m) 13 ft 1 in.

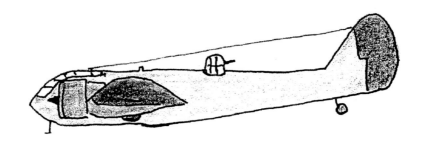

BRISTOL BLENHEIM MK1 -
UK Light 3 seater bomber of WWII.
2 - Engines - 840 hp Bristol Mercury VIII nine cylinder single row radial engines.
Max. speed - 285 mph (459 km)
Range - 1,125 mile (1810 km)
Weight - empty - 8,839 lbs (4,013 kg)
　　　　max. - 13,100 lbs (5,947 kg)
Wingspan - 56 ft 4" (17.17m)
Length - 39 ft 9" (12.12m)
Height - 9 ft 10" (3m)

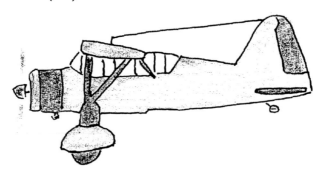

WESTLAND LYSANDER -
UK's main reconnaissance plane.
1 Engine - 890 hp Bristol Mercury XII nine cylinder single radial engine
Max. speed - 229 mph (369 km)
Range - 600 miles (966 km)
Weight empty - 4,065 lb (1,855 kg)
Wingspan - 50 ft (15,24m)
Length - 30'-6" (9,30m)
Height - 11 ft (3.35m)
Armament - 2 - 0. 303 machine guns in wheel fairings.
Further machine gun in rear cockpit.

DE HAVILLAND D.H. 82 TIGER MOTH -
Country of origin - UK. Used by the RAF from February 1932 and became the initial training plane of WW11. About 4,000 used between 1932 - 1947.
Engines - one 130 hp de Havilland Gypsy Major air-cooled inline.
Crew - two.
Max. Speed - 109 mph (176 km/h)
Range - 300 miles (482 km)
Ceiling - 14,000 ft (4,267 km)
Length - 23 ft 11 in (7.29 m)
Span - 29 ft 4 in (8.94m)
Height - 8 ft 9.5 in (2.66m)

ARMSTRONG WHITWORTH ALBEMARLE -
Medium bomber and only 600 were built. Primarily used for paratroops transport and glider tug.
Crew - three.
Engines - two 1590 hp Bristol Hercules X1 14 cylinder two-row radical engine.
Max. speed - 265 mph (426 km/h)
Range - 1300 miles (2092 km)
Ceiling - 18,000 ft (5485m)
Length - 59 ft 11 in. (18.26m)
Span - 77 ft (23.47m)
Height - 15 ft 7 in (4.75m)

Arthur Alexander Rubbra

Many of the crashed planes of British Combat aircraft during World War 11, were powered by Merlin engines, such as the Spitfire. The main person responsible for the engine was A.A. Rubbra, who lived in Derby. He worked for Rolls Royce for more than fifty years and in the 1920's worked on the Schneider Trophy engines. In the 1930's he became deputy chief designer to Rolls Royce aero division. He worked on the PV12 engine which later became the Merlin. The Lancaster bomber had four merlin engines. Rubbra had responsibility to improving the Merlin engine, which he did, always ahead of the German plane engines. Before the war the engine was 1,000 horsepower and by the end of the war it was more than double. His workload and responsibility at this time was said to be awesome but he was renowned for his quiet, skilled persistence. After the war he was responsible for the Griffon engine and the eagle - a big 24 cylinder engine. He moved in turbine engines. In 1954 he was Technical Director and worked from the Old Hall, Littleover, Derby, where research was carried out. Until 1966 he was deputy chairman of Rolls Royce, when he "retired" from fulltime work in 1968. The Royal Aeronautical Society awarded him their Gold Medal, in acknowledgement of his outstanding achievements.

If you are in Derby it is worth a visit to the Industrial Museum in the Old Silk Mill, to see a lot of information about the engines and Rolls Royce.

Derby Rolls-Royce Factory - There was only one air raid on the works, at 8.0 a.m. on Monday 27th. July 1942. A single Dorneir Do217E - 4 German bomber dropped four delayed action bombs on the factory. One hit the steel store and the three others landed around Hawthorne and Abingdon Street. 23 people were killed and more than 100 were injured.

The Dornier Do217 was a four seater two engined night fighter plane.

Some related interesting facts -

Whilst researching for this books the following facts have emerged.

- On July 11th 1912, the first plane to land in Derbyshire - a Bleriot - piloted by B.C.Hucks landed in Derby on the racecourse. The Bleriot was a monoplane built by Louis Bleriot, the French airman, who in 1909 became the first person to fly across the English Channel.

- On July 27th 1941 - A Daylight raid on Derby was made by a single aircraft.

- 17 bombs fell around Brassington one day during World War 11.

- In early Mach 1945 a lone German aircraft machine gunned Matlock and Belper.

- During three years of World War 11 the Buxton Mountain Rescue Unit helped at 88 crashed planes around Edale and Kinder.

- The ghosts of dead airmen are said to haunt Aston Lane in the Hope Valley.

- There are more than 40 crash sites in the Leek area, including a Junkers (German fighter plane) on the Roaches.

- Mr. F. Robinson of Matlock, remembers a single WW11 German plane firing over the town of Matlock. Bullets hit several buildings including Burgeon's, what is now the Derbyshire Building Scociety Matlock Branch. Here a window was smashed and the staff hung up a sign saying - *"Battle scarred but we carry on!"* Other buldings such as the Ritz Cinema (now Merlins) and Dakin's Newsagents were slightly damaged. A canon shell hit the Hall Leys park toilets.

- During WW11 a German fighter plane was on display in Beetwell Street, Chesterfield.

The two seater Bristol Fighter MK111, that crashed on Matlock Moor, July 16th. 1928.

DERBYSHIRE AIRFIELDS

The main airfield base for the area was at Lichfield, Staffordshire with satellite airfields at Ashbourne, Church Broughton, Darley Moor and Burnaston.

ASHBOURNE AIRFIELD - G.R. SK198455 - The site at 650 ft was inspected in 1941 and built to bomber airfields standard with three 50 yard wide runways - 1,700, 1,540 and 1,340 yards long. Work began in the Spring of 1941 and was in use from the summer of 1942 as a standard bomber air field. Because of frequent bad weather and Bomber Command reorganisations, the air field never became an operational bomber station. Initially part of Group 92 it was soon changed to the 93 Group with the Headquarters at Egginton Hall.

Almost immediately the airfield became a training one and the home of the 81 OTU - Operational Training Unit. At first 29 Wellington Bomber were allocated for crew training here, with plans to build a satellite airfield at Church Broughton, 8 miles to the south. The plans changed again Whitley's bombers were to be used instead of Wellington's. By October 1942 a new unit was established, the 420 OTU, and the first aircraft, a Westland Lysander arrived from southern England. The rest of the planes, Blenheims, Whitleys, Ansons and Oxford's arrived, together with more than 700 personnel.

The Blenheims and Whitley's were used for training the pilots and navigators and the Anson's and Oxford's for wireless and gunnery training. Nine crews a month were trained and sent for front line action. On the 5th. September 1943, a Armstrong Whitworth Abermarle landed at airfield, the first to be used as a training plane here. Many more arrived for preparation for D Day. The crews trained here and at Darley Moor were part of the invasion of Europe on June 6th. 1944. It is believed that a total of 1,400 aircrew were trained here and at Darley Moor.

On March 20th 1945 the unit was disbanded and the airfield closed to flying. The No. 28 Maintenance Unit was stationed here for the storage of bombs which were later exploded on the Derbyshire Moors. The station closed in 1954 and has since become an industrial estate.

CHURCH BROUGHTON - G.R. SK215320, 2 miles S.E. of Sudbury by the A50 - Started in 1942 and had three 50 yard wide runways. Many Australian crews were trained here. The airfield used Wellington's and sadly many crashed in the area with fatal results. Although the airfield basically closed in October 1944, it was used by Rolls Royce for jet engine testing purposes. In September 1945 the first flight of the Rolls Royce Trent powered Meteor took off from here. The airfield finally closed in July 1954.

DARLEY MOOR - G.R. SK175420 - 3 miles south of Ashbourne on the A515. A satellite airfield to Ashbourne with the 42 OTU arriving on the 26th. October 1942. The airfield closed on February 18th. 1945. The RAF still used the site for ammunition storage, but closed down completely on August 23rd. 1954.

BURNASTON AIRFIELD - G.R. SK290303 - 5 miles S.W. of Derby. Known as Derby Municipal Airport, being opened on Saturday 13th. June 1939. Served as a RAF Volunteer Reserve Training Centre. Basically Magister and Tiger Moth's were used here to train the pilots. Following the WW 11 the main base was transferred to Castle Donnington; today's Nottingham - East Midlands Airport. For a long while the airfield was used by the Derby Flying Club, until it became part of the Toyota car plant.

DERBYSHIRE FIGHTER PILOT'S

Derbyshire had several exceptional WW 11 pilots and perhaps the most renowned is Alan Feary. In Derby's Industrial Museum, there is a memorial to him, including his medals, close to a model Spitfire and Merlin engine. He shot down more than five German planes in combat and damaged many more.

OTHER CRASH SITES

Almost all the crash sites in the southern half of Derbyshire were during WW 11 by training crews from Ashbourne and Lichfield air fields or there satellite airfields. The numbers were high, partly due to mechanical problems or by inexperience. This was not necessarily the pilot's fault or crew, as training only lasted a few weeks before there were in a crew for Bomber Command. In fact reading this list and the other crashes on the different walks, you will soon realise that there were more crashes in the White Peak and South Derbyshire area than there was in the Dark Peak!

ASHBOURNE AIR FIELD -

The first accident, on November 7th. 1942. A Blenheim flown by Fg Off Mummery with LAC Clarke as crew hit a tree in the overshoot area. The plane burst into flames on hitting the ground, killing LAC Clarke and severely injuring, Fg Off Mummery.

January 1943 - A Blenheim suddenly lost height and all the crew were killed. A few days later another Blenheim had to make a forced landing and on this occasion no lives were lost.

July 8th 1943 - A Blenheim crashed killing the three crew. This was the last time Blenheim's were used for training at this airfield.

December 1944 - A Albemarle on returning from a night exercise, while on its final approach to the airfield, suddenly lost height and crashed into a house. The crew survived except for the navigator who was thrown ot of the plane on impact.

ALBEMARLE V-1610 - In 1944 it took off with a five man crew from RAF Ashbourne airfield. 80 minutes later it crashed at Kirton Fen, Lincolnshire, after being hit by a night-fighter. Of the five man crew only two were able to bale out. A plaque in 1992, was unveiled to the memory of the crash and crew at the Lincolnshire Aircraft Heritage Centre, East Kirkby. Remains of the plane are also on display there.

The monument near Weston Underwood is to the crew of a Whitley bomber that crashed here on July 24th. 1944. It was heading for Ashbourne airfield.

DARLEY MOOR AIRFIELD -

January 1943 - Oxford crash landed due to mechanical failure.

BURNASTON AIRFIELD -

January 3rd. 1939 - A Magister on its final approach crashed into the Rolls-Royce factory.

July 1940 - A Magister while practising its forced landing procedure, crashed at Darley Dale, near Matlock.

18th. August 1940 - A Magister while flying low over Royston, Derbyshire, hit some trees and crashed nearby. The pilot had been practising landings.

May 1941 - A Magister while practising spins over the airfield, spun out of control.

May 1941 - A Magister on taking off did not get sufficient height and crashed into trees at the end of the runway.

May 1941 - A Magister while over Sutton on Hill in Derbyshire, stalled and crashed.

November 1941 - A Magister suddenly dived into the ground at Repton, Derbyshire.

December 5th. 1941 - A Magister hit high ground at Atlow, destroying the plane.

December 8th. 1941 - A Magister while flying over Walton on Trent, Derbyshire lost a wing.

December 19th. 1941 - A Magister which was approaching the airfield too low, hit some trees.

A Miles Magister was a monoplane largely built of wood. Used mostly for training purposes.

February 26th. 1942 - A Magister was approaching Tatenhill, Staffs to land but stalled crashing into the ground.

February 26th. 1942 - A Magister was approaching Burnaston to land but hit a house nearby.

April 5th. 1942 - A Magister was making a landing run but crashed into another parked Magister.

April 1942 - A Magister was making a forced landing at Draycott but crashed.

May 22nd. 1942 - Another Magister was making a forced landing at Dalbury Lees but crashed.

1942 - Mickleover, Derby - a Tiger Moth went into a spin and the pilot was unable to correct it, crashed.

1942 - A Tiger Moth was practising forced landings at Walton on Trent when it crashed.

October 26th. 1943 - A Wellington bomber - HE696 - from Hixon, had been on a cross country training mission, attempted to make a landing at Burnaston airfield. The runway being short, the pilot ran out of runway and hit a hangar, killing one of the crew.

August 31st. 1944 - A Tiger Moth crashed in Chellaston, Derby, having collided with an Oxford.

MATLOCK MOOR CRASH - On July 16th. 1928, a Bristol Fighter MK111 - two seater biplane - Serial No. J8432. construction no. 6991, crashed on the moor, on the lane near the present day 11th. hole of the Matlock Golf Course - about G.R. 317622. The plane was manufactured on 17th. January 1927 and based at Henlow. Mr. Fred Hole of the nearby Wayside Farm remembers, when aged 12, visiting the crashed plane on his way home from Sunday school. It is believed the pilot, named Scott, had stayed at Rockside Hall (Hydro) in Matlock overnight. Shortly after taking off, he crashed and survived. He died two years later in another crash. I believe this is the first crash in Derbyshire? - the first in the Dark Peak was in 1937, a Heyford.

At the start of World War 11, Rockside Hydro (Hall), Matlock was requisitioned by the RAF for use as a hospital. To provide treatment and rest for airmen suffering from combat fatigue.

Photographs of the crashed plane appeared in the Matlock Mercury - January 29th. and February 26th. 2004. See front cover and last page for photographs of the crashed plane.

OTHER MATLOCK AREA CRASHES - An eye witness has informed me that a fighter plane crashed into the escarpment above the White Lion Inn, Starkholmes, Matlock.

BALK WOOD. GR 323589 - Another local recalls that an aircraft crashed during WW11 in the field opposite the road junction of Alders lane, Cunnery lane and Carr Lane (Riber Road). The site is almost midway between Dethick and Tansley. The plane hit the pine trees and for many years you could see the gap in the trees.

GLADWIN MARK. GR SK304667, near Beeley Moor. In 1941 a Wellington Bomber crashed here. The plane flying very low, at night, clipped the trees - you can still see the "stunted" pine trees here today, and crashed, killing all but one of the crew. *"Ten feet higher and they would have cleared the area".* I am indebted to an eye witness who provided me with this information. The pilot, covered in blood, arrived at Moor Farm, and the daughter of the house recalls, *"Her father was frightened to death",* at his arrival. Another witness recalls the rear gunner survived and jumped to the ground, breaking both legs. He crawled for help and eventually reached Moor Farm, on Flash Lane.

BONSALL - In the field beside Abel Lane, at Grid Ref. 273585 an aircraft crash landed during World War 11.

WESSINGTON - G.R. SK384583, near Mount Pleasant Farm. A Avro Anson in 1941 with engine trouble crash landed near the farm. As it landed it hit the farm drive before crashing into a hedge and field beyond. The crew survived and went back to Lincoln. The Home Guard watched over the plane before it was lifted by crane and dismantled, with the fuselage and wings loaded on trailers.

WELLINGTON BOMBER - Mickleover. So far I have been unable to find any details about this, except that the area is haunted by the ghosts of the airmen. Ghost stories are also told about an airman in Mickleover Hospital.

WELLINGTON BOMBER
- VI W5795 -
Crashed Stanley
- 12th. July 1942.

On Sunday, 12th. July 1942, a Wellington Bomber, piloted by Cyril Colmore, took off at 18.30 hr. from Boscombe Down. The plane was on a test flight being fitted with a new pilot's dome, known as D type, being a pressurised cabin for high altitude flying. The test was to carry out a full throttle ceiling climb to 35,500 feet. From that height it was to descend to various heights to carry out checks. After 55 minutes into the flight, all was proceeding as normal and the wireless operator, Gillott advised ground control that at 11,000 feet the cabin pressure was constant. Fifteen minutes later the plane was observed flying east over Derby and a local anti-aircraft battery plotted its course and height at 32,200 feet.

Suddenly there was a load bang and the plane went into a nose dive. As it descended the plane broke up and hit the ground around the village of Stanley, 4 1/2 miles north east of Derby, at 1941 hrs. All five crew were killed. The crash brought hoards of people out to see the wreckage that was strewn over a large area. Many of the lighter parts were brought to a central point which hampered the work of the Accident Investigation Branch (AIB) of the RAF. The wreckage was removed and taken back to Boscombe Down for examination.

The AIB pieced together the final moments of the flight. At 1935 hrs the plane was on full throttle, 2,850 r.p.m., at a height of 35,500 feet. Considerable vibration from the starboard engine, forced Colmore to throttle back and counteract the level position. This resulted in loss of cabin pressure and a major drop in cabin temperature. Five minutes later at 1940 hrs. the plane was on its descent at 32,200 ft. At this moment part of the blade of no. 4 starboard propellor broke off, hitting the cabin and fatally wounding Cyril Colmore, the pilot. He did try to stem the blood flow using his monogrammed handkerchief. He throttle back on the port engine before collapsing. Also injured was Abbot and Smith. Gillott attempted to reduce the cabin pressure to bail out but as the plane was now in a steep dive he was powerless. The hole in the cockpit got bigger as the plane descended and Abbot was sucked out. The port engine fell off and the plane began to break up, with the tail section first. Radford, the air gunner in the tail, had attempted to get out but again the speed of events overtook him.

Much of the wreckage fell in the Quarry Farm area of Stanley. Witnesses reported hearing three loud bangs and seeing one of the crew falling without a parachute; Abbot. On Monday a Spitfire circled the area and at night a group of soldiers from the West Hallam Depot, began searching for a missing crew member. He was found in a cornfield beside Stanley Hill.

Following the accident the Wellington was kept to a ceiling of 20,000 ft. and problems of stability at 30,000 feet still continued. The Wellington VI Bomber became known as "The flying coffin."

Crew -
Sqn Ldr. Cyril Colmore - Pilot
Plt. Officer Kenneth Radford - Air Gunner
Flt. Sgt. Arthur Smith - Navigator
Flt. Sgt. Ronald Gillott - Wireless Operator
Mr. Clifford Abbott - Flight Test Observer.

In Memory Of
The Crew Of Wellington Mk VI W5795
Who Tragically Lost Their Lives On
12th July 1942
In A Crash In The Quarry Farm Area Of This Parish

SQN LDR	CYRIL L. F. COLMORE	37651	RAF
PLT OFFR	KENNETH RADFORD	123492	RAFVR
FLT SGT	RONALD P. GILLOTT	650284	RAF
FLT SGT	ARTHUR J. SMITH	755349	DFM RAF
MR	CLIFFORD V. ABBOTT	CIV TEST OBSERVER	

WE WILL REMEMBER THEM

Memorial in Stanley churchyard; dedicated in July 2004.

Short Stirling Crash
Stanton by Dale
- August 31st. 1944

On August 31st. 1944 a Short Stirling - a four engined heavy bomber - crashed while on a training flight at Grove Farm (G.R. 454385) in the parish of Stanton by Dale, north-east of Derby. All seven members of the crew were killed. In the churchyard of Stanton by Dale church, dedicated to St. Michael and All Angels, are two plaques to the airmen. The war memorial, which I believe is a first in Derbyshire, has all names of the crew.

"And of the crew of the aircraft which crashed within the parish on 31 Aug 1944."

> R. Alexander Sgt
> P. Arthur F/Sgt
> W. Cox F/Sgt
> A. Hughes Sgt
> J. Lambell Sgt
> T. Westhead Sgt
> B.G. Wilkinson P/O

On the drive to the churchyard and church, part way up on the lefthand side, is a small plaque by a lampost. It reads -

"This lamp was made at Stanton Ironworks. It has been erected here on behalf of the pilot and the crew of a 630 Sqn Lancaster bomber as a memorial to their flight engineer, Flt Sgt Bill Cox DFM, later killed on a training flight in the Stirling aircraft crash at Grove Farm in this parish on 31st. August 1944."

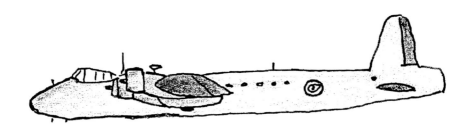

The British Short Stirling Aircraft was the first, specifically designed, four engined bomber, and the Mk 1 began service in August 1940. Altogether 2,374 aircraft were built. The Mk 1V version was a paratroop and glider towing aircraft and the Mk V was used as unarmed transport.

Crew- seven or eight.
Engines - four 1650 hp Bristol Hercules XV1 14 cylinder two-row radical engine.
Max. speed - 270 mph.
Service ceiling - 17,000 feet.
Range - 2,010 miles. when carrying 3,500 bomb load.
Weight - empty 46,900 lbs with a maximum take off weight of 70,000 lbs.
Dimensions - Wing span 99 ft 1 inches - the Air Ministry had instructed that it should be under 100 feet. Length - 87 feet 3 in and 22 ft 9 in high.
Armaments - Nose Turret - two 0.303 forward firing machine guns.
Dorsal Turret - two 0.303 trainable machine guns.
Tail Turret - four o.303 trainable rearward firing machine guns.
Internal bomb load was a maximum of 14,000 lbs.

ALSO TO THE MEMORY OF
THE FOLLOWING MEN OF
STANTON - BY - DALE WHO
GAVE THEIR LIVES IN THE
WAR 1939 - 1945

H.W. BROOK   Sgt.   24 NOV. 1940.
A. WOOD   O/S.   2 OCT. 1942.
K.W. KING   CPL.   27 OCT. 1942.
T.W.H. USHER F/Sgt. 6 FEB. 1945.
AND OF THE CREW OF THE
AIRCRAFT WHICH CRASHED
WITHIN THE PARISH ON 31 AUG 1944

R. ALEXANDER   Sgt.
P. ARTHUR   F/Sgt.
W. COX   F/Sgt.
A. HUGHES   Sgt.
J. LAMBELL   Sgt.
T. WESTHEAD   Sgt.
R.G. WILKINSON P/O.

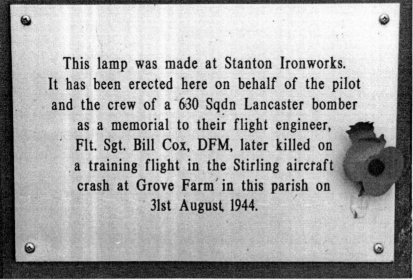

This lamp was made at Stanton Ironworks.
It has been erected here on behalf of the pilot
and the crew of a 630 Sqdn Lancaster bomber
as a memorial to their flight engineer,
Flt. Sgt. Bill Cox, DFM, later killed on
a training flight in the Stirling aircraft
crash at Grove Farm in this parish on
31st August, 1944.

Plaques to the crew of the Short Stirling in Stanton by Dale churchyard.

Some Reference Sources and Further reading -

The Dambusters Raid by John Sweetman

The Dambusters Squadron - 50 years of the 617 Squadron RAF by Alan Cooper

A Moorlands Dedication - *an account of the 40 military aircraft accidents in the Leek area of North Staffordshire during World War 11* by Marshall S. Boylan.

A few of the Derbyshire "few" - Derbyshire Fighter Pilots in WW 11 by Barry M. Marsden.

The Burnaston Story by M. Giddings

Notthamshire and Derbyshire Airfields by Robin J. Brooks

Bygone Aircraft - Derby Evening Telegraph - Summer 1989.

Aircraft of World War 11 by Chris Chant

Warolanes of the Luftwaffe -edited by David Donald.

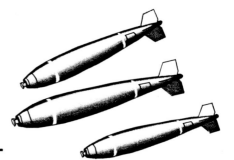

UNEXPLODED BOMBS -

It seems almost amazingly that unexploded bombs are still being found in the Peak District, some sixty years after World War 11. The Eastern Moors, as a decoy for German bombers bound for Sheffield and its steel works, were lit up and many crews dropped their bombs believing it was Sheffield. A walker on White Edge in April 2004, discovered a bomb which had become exposed because of the erosion of the path. A bomb disposal team from Nottingham was immediately sent and the mortar bomb had a controlled explosion. The landlady of the nearby Grouse Inn said, "The whole thing was very exciting. We saw this great rush of smoke followed by a large explosion, then there was a mass rush of sheep and lambs."

WHITE PEAK WALK - AIRCRAFT CRASH LOCATIONS

PLANE	CRASH DATE	LOCATION	GRID REF.
Thunderbolts (2)	10/10/1944(?)	Cats Tor	SK995754
Wellington No Z1744	11/11/1944	Hen Cloud	SK008614
Seafires (2)		Birchenough Hill	SK99-676-
B17 Flying Fortress No. 43 - 38944	2/01/1945	Birchenough Hill	SK995678
Junkers 88	08/05/1941	Moss End Farm	SK004648
Halifax Bomber No. RT 922 F	13/02/1947	Grindon Moor	SK063553
Boulton Paul Defiant - T3921	16/10/1941	Shining Tor	SK998738
Airspeed Oxford - LX745	12/03/1944	Shining Tor	SK99-73-
North American Harvard - FT442	30/11/1944	Shining Tor	SK002738
Avro Lancaster - NF908	03/01/1945	The Roaches	SK002636
Supermarine Spitfire- P7593	17/11/1940	The Roaches	SK00-63-
Miles Master - W8840	15/01/1943	Near Leek	
Airspeed Oxford - L4601	14/04/1945	Shutlingsloe	SK97-69-
De Havilland Vampire - WA400	25/07/1951	Strines Moor	SK218899
De Havilland Vampre - XE866	08/08/1957	Moscar Moor	SK224857
Vickers Wellington - MF627	22/10/1952	Rod Moor	SK264893
Vickers Wellington - BJ652	21/01/1944	Smerrill Grange	SK199618
Whitley Bomber	14/07/1944	Weston Underwood	SK295439

73

WALK RECORD CHART

Walks -

Rod Moor - 5 miles ....

Stanedge - Crow Chin - 4 miles ....

Over Haddon , Conksbury and Youlgreave - 4 miles ....

Middleton and Smerrill - 6 miles ....

Shining Tor - 6 to 8 miles ....

Shutlingsloe - 4 miles ....

Gradbach - 6 miles ....

The Roaches - 5 miles ....

Grindon Moor - 7 miles ....

Weston Underwood - 5 miles ....

Derwent Dams -Dam Busters Walk - 10 miles ....

Hulland Ward and Bradley - 7 1/2 miles..

JOHN MERRILL WALK BADGE

THE JOHN MERRILL WALK BADGE

Complete six walks in this book and get the above special embroidered badge and signed certificate. Badges are Blue cloth with lettering and hiker embroidered in four colours.

BADGE ORDER FORM

Date walks completed...

NAME ....

ADDRESS ....

....

Price: £4.50 each including postage, packing, VAT and signed completion certificate. Amount enclosed (Payable to Walk & Write Ltd) ..
From: Walk & Write Ltd.,
Marathon House, Longcliffe,
Nr. Matlock, Derbyshire. DE4 4HN
Tel /Fax 01629 - 540991
+++++++++++ YOU MAY PHOTOCOPY THIS FORM   +++++++++++

"HAPPY WALKING!" T SHIRT
- Yellow (daisy) with black lettering and walking man logo.
Send £8.95 to Walk & Write Ltd., stating size required.
Happy walking embroidered, full length zipped, Fleece Jacket - £17.95

Companion volume -

AIRCRAFT WRECK WALKS SERIES

DARK PEAK AIRCRAFT WRECK WALKS

by John N. Merrill

OTHER JOHN MERRILL WALK BOOKS

CIRCULAR WALK GUIDES -
SHORT CIRCULAR WALKS IN THE PEAK DISTRICT - Vol. 1,2 and 3
CIRCULAR WALKS IN WESTERN PEAKLAND
SHORT CIRCULAR WALKS IN THE STAFFORDSHIRE MOORLANDS
SHORT CIRCULAR WALKS - TOWNS & VILLAGES OF THE PEAK DISTRICT
SHORT CIRCULAR WALKS AROUND MATLOCK
SHORT CIRCULAR WALKS IN "PEAK PRACTICE COUNTRY."
SHORT CIRCULAR WALKS IN THE DUKERIES
SHORT CIRCULAR WALKS IN SOUTH YORKSHIRE
SHORT CIRCULAR WALKS IN SOUTH DERBYSHIRE
SHORT CIRCULAR WALKS AROUND BUXTON
SHORT CIRCULAR WALKS AROUND WIRKSWORTH
SHORT CIRCULAR WALKS IN THE HOPE VALLEY
40 SHORT CIRCULAR WALKS IN THE PEAK DISTRICT
CIRCULAR WALKS ON KINDER & BLEAKLOW
SHORT CIRCULAR WALKS IN SOUTH NOTTINGHAMSHIRE
SHORT CIRCULAR WALKS IN CHESHIRE
SHORT CIRCULAR WALKS IN WEST YORKSHIRE
WHITE PEAK DISTRICT AIRCRAFT WRECKS
CIRCULAR WALKS IN THE DERBYSHIRE DALES
SHORT CIRCULAR WALKS FROM BAKEWELL
SHORT CIRCULAR WALKS IN LATHKILL DALE
CIRCULAR WALKS IN THE WHITE PEAK
SHORT CIRCULAR WALKS IN EAST DEVON
SHORT CIRCULAR WALKS AROUND HARROGATE
SHORT CIRCULAR WALKS IN CHARNWOOD FOREST
SHORT CIRCULAR WALKS AROUND CHESTERFIELD
SHORT CIRCULAR WALKS IN THE YORKS DALES - Vol 1 - Southern area.
SHORT CIRCULAR WALKS IN THE AMBER VALLEY (Derbyshire)
SHORT CIRCULAR WALKS IN THE LAKE DISTRICT
SHORT CIRCULAR WALKS IN THE NORTH YORKSHIRE MOORS
SHORT CIRCULAR WALKS IN EAST STAFFORDSHIRE
DRIVING TO WALK - 16 Short Circular walks south of London by Dr. Simon Archer Vol 1 and 2
LONG CIRCULAR WALKS IN THE PEAK DISTRICT - Vol.1,2 ,3 and 4.
DARK PEAK AIRCRAFT WRECK WALKS
LONG CIRCULAR WALKS IN THE STAFFORDSHIRE MOORLANDS
LONG CIRCULAR WALKS IN CHESHIRE
WALKING THE TISSINGTON TRAIL
WALKING THE HIGH PEAK TRAIL
WALKING THE MONSAL TRAIL & OTHER DERBYSHIRE TRAILS
PEAK DISTRICT WALKING - TEN "TEN MILER'S" - Vol One and Two
CLIMB THE PEAKS OF THE PEAK DISTRICT
PEAK DISTRICT WALK A MONTH Vols One,Two, Three, and Four
TRAIN TO WALK Vol. One - The Hope Valley Line
DERBYSHIRE LOST VILLAGE WALKS -Vol One and Two.
CIRCULAR WALKS IN DOVEDALE AND THE MANIFOLD VALLEY
CIRCULAR WALKS AROUND GLOSSOP
WALKING THE LONGDENDALE TRAIL
WALKING THE UPPER DON TRAIL
SHORT CIRCULAR WALKS IN CANNOCK CHASE
CIRCULAR WALKS IN THE DERWENT VALLEY
WALKING THE TRAILS OF NORTH-EAST DERBYSHIRE

CANAL WALKS -
VOL 1 - DERBYSHIRE & NOTTINGHAMSHIRE
VOL 2 - CHESHIRE & STAFFORDSHIRE
VOL 3 - STAFFORDSHIRE
VOL 4 - THE CHESHIRE RING
VOL 5 - LINCOLNSHIRE & NOTTINGHAMSHIRE
VOL 6 - SOUTH YORKSHIRE
VOL 7 - THE TRENT & MERSEY CANAL
VOL 8 - WALKING THE DERBY CANAL RING
VOL 9 - WALKING THE LLANGOLLEN CANAL
VOL 10 - CIRCULAR WALKS ON THE CHESTERFIELD CANAL

JOHN MERRILL DAY CHALLENGE WALKS -
WHITE PEAK CHALLENGE WALK
THE HAPPY HIKER - WHITE PEAK - CHALLENGE WALK No.2
DARK PEAK CHALLENGE WALK
PEAK DISTRICT END TO END WALKS
STAFFORDSHIRE MOORLANDS CHALLENGE WALK
THE LITTLE JOHN CHALLENGE WALK
YORKSHIRE DALES CHALLENGE WALK

NORTH YORKSHIRE MOORS CHALLENGE WALK
LAKELAND CHALLENGE WALK
THE RUTLAND WATER CHALLENGE WALK
MALVERN HILLS CHALLENGE WALK
THE SALTER'S WAY
THE SNOWDON CHALLENGE
CHARNWOOD FOREST CHALLENGE WALK
THREE COUNTIES CHALLENGE WALK (Peak District).
CAL-DER-WENT WALK by Geoffrey Carr,
THE QUANTOCK WAY
BELVOIR WITCHES CHALLENGE WALK
THE CARNEDDAU CHALLENGE WALK
THE SWEET PEA CHALLENGE WALK
THE LINCOLNSHIRE WOLDS - BLACK DEATH - CHALLENGE WALK

INSTRUCTION & RECORD -
HIKE TO BE FIT.....STROLLING WITH JOHN
THE JOHN MERRILL WALK RECORD BOOK
HIKE THE WORLD

MULTIPLE DAY WALKS -
THE RIVERS'S WAY
PEAK DISTRICT: HIGH LEVEL ROUTE
PEAK DISTRICT MARATHONS
THE LIMEY WAY
THE PEAKLAND WAY
COMPO'S WAY by Alan Hiley
THE BRIGHTON WAY by Norman Willis

THE PILGRIM WALKS SERIES -
THE WALSINGHAM WAY - Ely to Walsingham - 72 miles
THE WALSINGHAM WAY - Kings Lynn to Walsingham - 35 miles
TURN LEFT AT GRANJA DE LA MORERUELA - 700 miles
NORTH TO SANTIAGO DE COMPOSTELA, VIA FATIMA - 650 miles
St. OLAV'S WAY - Oslo to Trondheim - 400 miles

COAST WALKS & NATIONAL TRAILS -
ISLE OF WIGHT COAST PATH
PEMBROKESHIRE COAST PATH
THE CLEVELAND WAY
WALKING ANGELSEY'S COASTLINE.
WALKING THE COASTLINE OF THE CHANNEL ISLANDS

DERBYSHIRE & PEAK DISTRICT HISTORICAL GUIDES -
A to Z GUIDE OF THE PEAK DISTRICT
DERBYSHIRE INNS - an A to Z guide
HALLS AND CASTLES OF THE PEAK DISTRICT & DERBYSHIRE
TOURING THE PEAK DISTRICT & DERBYSHIRE BY CAR
DERBYSHIRE FOLKLORE
PUNISHMENT IN DERBYSHIRE
CUSTOMS OF THE PEAK DISTRICT & DERBYSHIRE
WINSTER - a souvenir guide
ARKWRIGHT OF CROMFORD
LEGENDS OF DERBYSHIRE
DERBYSHIRE FACTS & RECORDS
TALES FROM THE MINES by Geoffrey Carr
PEAK DISTRICT PLACE NAMES by Martin Spray
DERBYSHIRE THROUGH THE AGES - Vol 1 -DERBYSHIRE IN PREHISTORIC TIMES
SIR JOSEPH PAXTON
FLORENCE NIGHTINGALE
JOHN SMEDLEY
BONNIE PRINCE CHARLIE & 20 mile walk.

JOHN MERRILL'S MAJOR WALKS -
TURN RIGHT AT LAND'S END
WITH MUSTARD ON MY BACK
TURN RIGHT AT DEATH VALLEY
EMERALD COAST WALK
JOHN MERRILL'S 1999 WALKER'S DIARY
A WALK IN OHIO - 1,310 miles around the Buckeye Trail.

SKETCH BOOKS -
SKETCHES OF THE PEAK DISTRICT

COLOUR BOOK:-
THE PEAK DISTRICT.......something to remember her by.

OVERSEAS GUIDES -
HIKING IN NEW MEXICO - Vol I - The Sandia and Manzano Mountains.
Vol 2 - Hiking "Billy the Kid" Country. Vol 4 - N.W. area - " Hiking Indian Country."
"WALKING IN DRACULA COUNTRY" - Romania.

VISITOR GUIDES - MATLOCK . BAKEWELL. ASHBOURNE.

Visit my showroom and see the whole range of my books and walking memorbilia at Marathon House, Longcliffe, Nr. Matlock, Derbyshire.

78

John Merrill's
"My Derbyshire" Historical Series.

A TO Z GUIDE TO THE PEAK DISTRICT by John N. Merrill
WINSTER - A SOUVENIR GUIDE .by John N. Merrill
DERBYSHIRE INNS - an A TO Z GUIDE . by John N. Merrill
HALLS & CASTLES OF THE PEAK DISTRICT. by John N. Merrill.
DERBYSHIRE FACTS AND RECORDS by John N. Merrill
THE STORY OF THE EYAM PLAGUE by Claence Daniel
THE EYAM DISCOVERY TRAIL by Clarence Daniel
PEAK DISTRICT SKETCHBOOKby John N. Merrill
LOST DERBYSHIRE VILLAGE WALKS - VOL 1 & 2 by John N. Merrill
TOURING THE PEAK DISTRICY & DERBYSHIRE BY CAR by John N. Merrill
LOST INDUSTRIES OF DERBYSHIRE by John N. Merrill
DESERTED MEDIEVAL VILLAGES OF DERBYSHIRE by John N. Merrill
MANORS & FAMILIES OF DERBYSHIRE - Vol 1 - A to L
MANORS & FAMILES OF DERBYSHIRE -Vol 2 - M to Z

FAMOUS DERBYSHIRE PEOPLE -
SIR RICHARD ARKWRIGHT OF CROMFORD by John N. Merrill.
SIR JOSEPH PAXTON by John N. Merrill
FLORENCE NIGHTINGALE by John N. Merrill
JOHN SMEDLEY by John N. Merrill
MARY QUEEN OF SCOTS - "The Captive Queen." by John N. Merrill
BESS OF HARDWICK - "The Costly Countess" by John N. Merrill
THE EARLS AND DUKES OF DEVONSHIRE by John N. Merrill
BONNIE PRINCE CHARLIE & 20 mile walk by John N. Merrill

GHOSTS & LEGENDS -
DERBYSHIRE FOLKLORE.by John N. Merrill.
DERBYSHIRE PUNISHMENT by John N. Merrill.
CUSTOMS OF THE PEAK DISTRICT & DERBYS by John N. Merrill
LEGENDS OF DERBYSHIRE. by John N. Merrill.
GRANDFATHER THOMAS JACKSON'S VICTORIAN CURES & RECIPES
DERBYSHIRE PILGRIMS & PILGRIMAGE'S by John N. Merrill

PEAK DISTRICT VISITOR'S GUIDES by John N. Merrill
ASHOURNE   BAKEWELL   MATLOCK   THE HOPE VALLEY

DERBYSHIRE HISTORY THROUGH THE AGES -
Vol 1 - DERBYSHIRE IN PREHISTORIC TIMES & 13 mile walk by John N. Merrill
Vol 3 - DERBYSHIRE IN NORMAN TIMES by John N. Merrill
Vol 4 - DERBYSHIRE IN MONASTIC TIMES by John N. Merrill

The Matlock Moor Crash - Bristol Fighter MK111. Taken from a postcard printed by Harry Gill, on the back was written - "Came down at Matlock Moor, July 16th. 1928. I am indebted to Peter and Anne Barker of Matlock, who allowed me reproduce their postcard, which they found in Anne's late Grandfather's belongings.

B17 Flying Fortress Wreckage at Grid Ref 997677
- see Gradbach Walk, page 32-35.

HULLAND WARD AND BRADLEY
- 7 1/2 MILES

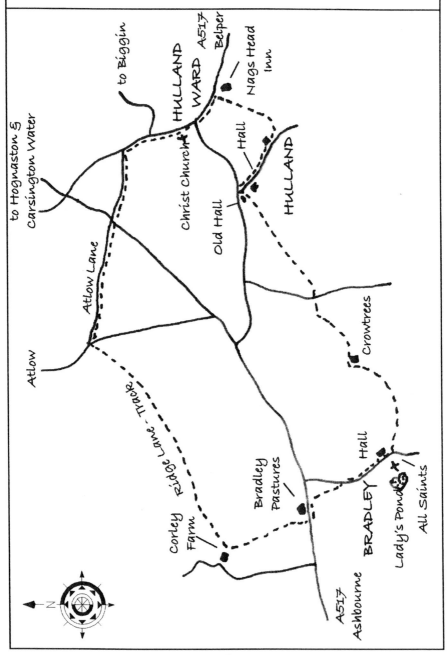

HULLAND WARD AND BRADLEY
- 7 1/2 MILES
- allow 3 hours

Basic route - Hulland Ward - Atlowtop - Ridge Lane - Corley Farm - Bradley Pastures - A517 - Bradley - Crowtrees - Lower Hough Park - Hulland - Hulland Ward - A517.

Map - O.S. 1:25,000 Explorer Series No. 259 - Derby.

Car Park and start - Limited roadside parking on Dog Lane, Hulland Ward, beside the church dedicated to Christ Church. Just off the A517 - Belper-Ashbourne Road, at G.R. 249474.

Inn - Nags Head, Hulland Ward.

ABOUT THE WALK - This is a little walked area of Derbyshire, to the east of Ashbourne. The paths and tracks are well stiled and signed. The views are extensive especially from Ridge Lane towards Ashbourne and beyond. The walk has several themes; one being you can visit both Hulland Ward and Bradley churches which have plaques to W.W. 11 pilots and crews. Secondly you visit two surprising villages, Bradley and Hulland with impressive halls and where time has passed by leaving treasures to see for the intrepid walker.

There are very few graves or plaques to W.W. 11 Pilots and crews in Derbyshire. On this walk in two small churches you can see plaques to them. Although not on this walk, if you have time it is worth visiting St. James church, Idridgehay, which has in the far churchyard three individual RAF graves - see photos.

WALKING INSTRUCTIONS - Starting from Christ Church, Hulland Ward, on Dog Lane, walk away from the village towards Hognaston. Pass the road to Biggin on your right and soon afterwards at Nether Flatts Cottage on the right, turn left onto the Atlow Road - a lane. In more than 1/4 mile cross another road, keeping straight ahead on the Atlow road (Atlow Lane). Pass Atlowtop on the right and views north to Harborough Rocks. At the next road junction turn half left to a hedged track - Ridge Lane. Keep on this for the next 3/4 mile with views in every direction as you walk along. Reaching a gate the track turns right, keep straight ahead now on path line by a hedge on your left. Reach a wooden stile and begin descending by the field hedge on your left to two more stiles before crossing a footbridge in the bottom. Ascend beyond to being level with Corley Farm on your right. Turn left keeping the fence on your right to a gate. Keep straight ahead descending slightly to another footbridge. Continue ahead ascending gently close to the righthand side of the field. At the top turn left and in a few yards right over a stile into woodland with a pond to your right. Keep straight ahead into the next field and continue by the hedge on the right to a gate and the A517 road.

Turn left and in a few yards pass Bradley Pastures on the left and a few yards later, turn right at the stile and path sign. Cross the field and take the lefthand gap to continue with a hedge on the right at first. Soon pass the lefthand side of a row of houses and cross the next field to a cattle grid and track before the Bradley road. Turn right into Bradley passing the large hall on the left and the small church of All Saints on the right. Beyond is Lady's Pond. Continue along the lane to the school and telephone kiosk. Turn left onto a drive and follow this for the next 1/2 mile, crossing two cattle grids and a house on your left. As you approach Crowtrees, turn left to walk around the fenced grounds to your right, to two gates on its lefthand side. In the field after the second gate walk halfway through the field to the middle lefthand side and a gate gap. Bearing half left cross two fields as you slightly descend to a stile. Bear right to two more stiles and the lane near Lower Hough Park. Cross to a gate and keeping to the lefthand side of the field soon gain another gate on the left in trees. Cross the field beyond to a small stream and onto a stile and footbridge. Ascend and turn left to a stile on the immediate right of woodland. Continue with the woodland on your left at first before leaving it and bearing slightly right to the next stile. Keep straight ahead to a stile by a solitary tree and gain a track. Turn left and follow it to Hulland Lane. Gaining the road on your left is the Old Hall of Hulland. Turn right along the lane passing Hulland Hall. In five minutes pass The Firs on the left. Just after turn left, as path signed and follow the path past the houses on the right. The path soon turns sharp right; here keep straight ahead on another path in woodland. In 100 yards turn left to continue beside a hedge on your left to reach a stile in the far lefthand corner of the field. Cross to another and onto the next one before walking between the houses to the A517 road in Hulland Ward. Opposite is The Sheiling and to your right the Nags Head Inn. Turn left then right into Dog Lane.

BRADLEY - The church dedicated to All Saints dates from the 14th century and is unusual in not having tower. Inside is a stone believed to show Adam and Eve. Bradley Hall was originally built from stables which had been built for another house

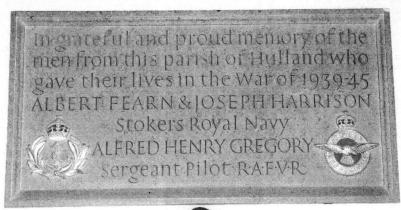

Plaque in Christ Church, Hulland Ward.

CHRIST CHURCH, HULLAND WARD - Built in 1838 at a cost of £2,300.

1939   1945

F/O ROBERT TOMLINSON
R·A·F·V·R
4TH JUNE 1943

Greater love hath no man than this.

Plaque in All Saints church, Bradley.

HULLAND - The Old Hall was built from stone from the demolished Manor House in 1692. The present Hulland Hall was built in 1777 by John Tempest Borrow. This family gave the land for the church at Hulland Ward.

W.W.11 RAF graves in St. James churchyard, Idridgehay

W.W.11 RAF graves in St. James churchyard, Idridgehay

AIRCRAFT MUSEUMS AND VISITOR'S CENTRE

Newark (Notts & Lincs) Air Museum,
Winthorpe Airfield,
Newark,
Notts.
NG24 2NY

Tel. 01636 - 707170
Has a large range of planes including a Vulcan, Avro Anson, Tiger Moth, and Gloster Meteor. Plus wreckage and engines from a Junkers, Wellington, Lancaster and Halifax.

Battle of Britain Memorial Flight Centre Visitor Centre,
RAF Coningsby,
Lincolnshire
LN4 4SY

Tel. 01526 - 344041
Has a Lancaster, Spitfires, Hurricanes and a Dakota; all of which are maintained and still fly.

Metheringham Airfield Visitor Centre,
Westmoor Farm,
Martin Moor,
Metheringham,
Lincolnshire.
LN4 3BQ

Tel. 01526 - 378270
Museum, Visitor's Centre, Memorial Gardens and flybys.

The Lincolnshire Aviation Heritage Centre,
East Kirkby,
Nr. Spilsby,
Lincolnshire.

Tel - 10790 - 763207
Situated on a 1940's Bomber airfield. Avro Lancaster Bomber and the Barnes Wallis Bouncing Bomb. Visitor Centre.